LOW-BUDGET ONLINE MARKETING FOR SMALL BUSINESS

LOW-BUDGET ONLINE MARKETING FOR SMALL BUSINESS

Holly Berkley

Self-Counsel Press
(a division of)
International Self-Counsel Press
USA   Canada

Self-Counsel Press acknowledges the financial support of the Government of Canada through the Book Publishing Industry Development Program (BPIDP) for our publishing acitivities.

Printed in Canada.

First edition: 2003
Second edition: 2005

Library and Archives Canada Cataloguing in Publication

Berkley, Holly
    Low-budget online marketing for small business / Holly Berkley. — 2nd ed.

(Self-counsel business series)
Includes bibliographical references.
ISBN 1-55180-634-7

    1. Internet marketing. 2. Small business—Computer networks. I. Title. II. Series.
    HF5415.1265.B47 2005   658.8'4   C2005-901355-9

Self-Counsel Press
(a division of)
International Self-Counsel Press Ltd.

1704 North State Street	1481 Charlotte Road
Bellingham, WA 98225	North Vancouver, BC V7J 1H1
USA	Canada

To my husband, Keith, and my friend Amanda, for their unconditional support and encouragement along my career path. And to my parents, Judy and Bill Betts, and my brother, Billy, for their support throughout life.

And to all the small-business owners and entrepreneurs out there who have dedicated their passion, hard work, and drive to make their ideas a reality. May your businesses be profitable and rewarding.

CONTENTS

WORKSHEETS

INTRODUCTION

After working for high-priced web design and advertising agencies, I learned firsthand just how much money some businesses are willing to spend to market their products and services over the Internet. Having big budgets to play with is great. Spending money is easy. With a big budget behind you, marketing your business online is pretty straightforward. However, if you have a limited budget but expect similar results, successful online marketing takes some creative thinking.

When I started my own web design and online marketing company in 1999, I was forced to find low-cost ways to give my small-business clients the same type of services I offered the big-budget clients at the agency. I started looking for ways to replicate the six-figure marketing campaigns for small businesses. The Internet is the perfect medium for this, because you can test ads and concepts for a fraction of the cost of print, radio, or television ads.

Advertising on the web is extremely targeted and measurable, making it the most cost-effective form of advertising available today. There is no other medium that allows small businesses to truly compete with the big guys.

This book provides online marketing case studies of top companies such as Pepsi-Cola, Banana Republic, Jenny Craig International, BMW, and Amazon.com, then explains how you can create similar campaigns for much less. You will learn how to generate quality website traffic and sales leads while saving money at the same time. I will show you how to turn a website into a trusted resource and how to entice customers to frequent your online store.

This book does not explain how to set up an e-business, but rather how to improve the marketing efforts of an existing business. It is for any group or individual hoping to market an idea, company, service, or product with limited resources and funds. Through it, you will learn —

- how to ensure that your company website is designed to specifically attract your ideal customer,

- how to use e-mail marketing to reach potential customers,

- the importance of co-branding and how to choose the right online partners,

- how to create custom content that keeps your audience coming back for more,

- how to position yourself as an authority in your industry, and

- how to spend your marketing dollars wisely with cost-effective ad buys and search engine registration techniques that will put your website ahead of its competitors.

This book will give you the information you need to take high-end online marketing and web design concepts and make them work for your business and your budget.

CHAPTER 1

THE BENEFITS OF ONLINE MARKETING

What's the difference between a $100,000 online marketing campaign and a $1,000 campaign? Surprisingly, not much. Sure, the six-figure campaign might have flashier graphics, well-known celebrities, or a more sophisticated database to store and track all the market data, but the concepts behind the two campaigns are almost identical.

The rules of marketing are the same for any size of business: establish your brand, find your target audience, generate sales, and encourage repeat business. The web lets you do all of these things for about one-tenth the cost of print and about one-thousandth the cost of television.

What Is Online Marketing?

So what exactly is online marketing? Online marketing is the process of putting your product or business in front of more than 200 million regular Internet users looking for services and information online. It is the process of turning your current website into a powerful medium to maximize your business and sales potential.

Online marketing is much more than buying ads online. It's about how you communicate with your customers via e-mail, message boards, and chatrooms. It is about updating your website with important product information and offers. It is any kind of promotion your company does using the Internet.

The center of your online marketing efforts should be your website. The feelings consumers have when they visit your website carry over to how they perceive your entire company or organization. No matter how effective your marketing campaign is, if you don't have a well-designed, professional-looking website, people will not buy from you. (See chapter 10 for details on improving the design of your website.)

The advantage of online marketing is that you don't have to have a multimillion-dollar marketing budget to put together an effective campaign. There are now shopping cart templates, website templates, and even online marketing templates created by companies such as Yahoo! and MSN that help companies with limited budgets get their e-business quickly off the ground. Also, because there is so much competition between web designers and programmers right now, if you know the right questions to ask (see chapter 11 on working with web developers), you can take very sophisticated online marketing strategies and implement them on almost any size budget.

Prerequisites for Successful Online Marketing

Before getting into the details and strategies of online marketing, here are some important factors to consider, among them human resources, the importance of consistent communication, and the need to buy online.

Adequate human resources

First, to succeed online, you must have real people working behind your website. No matter how sophisticated technology gets, websites don't run themselves. It is the personal touches and quick responses to problems that make a website work and turn visitors into customers.

The standard acceptable time to return a business e-mail is 48 to 72 hours. Take any longer than that and you have most likely lost the customer. If you do not have the human resources to return e-mails in two to three business days, you need to rethink your online marketing strategy. Although there are several e-mail automation programs, you cannot depend on automated responses to answer your customer's specific questions. Customers are still looking for that human touch, even through a computer monitor.

My husband and I learned this firsthand when we decided to start a travel website dedicated to Baja California, Mexico. Through our website, we offered services such as Mexican auto insurance (a necessity for any American driving across the border), hotel and airline reservations, and special products from Mexico such as clothing and artwork. We honestly thought that by posting a vast amount of information on our website such as travel tips, local events, laws, and so on, customers would get all the information they needed about traveling in Baja and the site would essentially run itself. We planned to travel Mexico while we watched the money from our website roll in. We couldn't have been more wrong.

No matter how many links and stories we posted, we still received hundreds of e-mails from customers wanting more information — especially when it came to making a purchase. We were even reprimanded on our own message boards for not answering posts on a regular basis!

We learned right away that building a website does not eliminate the need for customer service. In fact, it should allow you to give better customer service. A common misconception exists among companies that creating a website replaces customer service. Although websites do help customers find information they need about your product or service, in the process, they can actually create a need for more human resources.

Websites do not eliminate the need for customer service; they should enable you to give better customer service.

Consistent communication

How you reply to a customer's e-mail is an extremely important part of online marketing. If you've spent the time and money to get a customer to look at your website, then contact you, it would be a shame to lose that potential customer just at the time when you could be closing a sale. E-mail is a cheap and highly effective way to generate and close sales, but consistency is key. Be sure your e-mails carry the same tone as your website. For example, if your website is fun and humorous, your e-mails should be written that way. If your company has a very corporate, serious brand, your e-mails should convey an equally professional tone.

Your brand should carry over to all your online communications, right down to your e-mail signature. In most e-mail programs, you can set up a personal e-mail signature that will automatically attach to all of your outgoing messages. All of your e-mails, whether sent to business associates, clients, or friends, should be signed with your business signature. An effective e-mail signature should include your full name, title, contact info, website address, and a couple of words explaining what you do. You can even add a couple of lines about a company promotion.

Here are some examples of good e-mail signatures:

Holly Berkley
Berkley Web Strategies, LLC
Online Marketing & Website Design
555-555-5555
www.berkweb.com
Subscribe to my e-mail newsletter for monthly online marketing tips and discounts on website design services. Join now!

Doug Lewis
System Administrator
Vantage Internet
555-555-5555
www.VantageInternet.com
Refer a friend and get 1 month free hosting!

Jennifer Nichols
Tria Advertising, Marketing & Special Events
555-555-5555
www.triaadvertising.com
September Special: Get 500 business cards for $99.

Keith Berkley
Berkley Homes
International Land Development
License # 833169
555-555-5555
www.berkhome.com
Let us help you build your dream home in a foreign country!

A product consumers need to buy online

After the customer service commitment, the second most important factor to consider before starting an online marketing campaign is whether or not there exists a reasonable need for your product or service to be available online. Customers must find genuine value in buying something through your website, rather than dropping by the local mall or convenience store.

Genuine value really boils down to two key motivating factors:

▶ Convenience

▶ Cost

Is your product rare or hard to find in your area? Is it easier for customers to buy your product online than to drive to a local store? Is it cheaper to sell the product over the Internet than in a storefront?

A perfect example of e-tailers cashing in on a consumer need based on convenience and cost occurred when the new tobacco tax was enacted in New York in autumn 2002. The tobacco tax sent the cost of cigarettes skyrocketing to more than $7.50 a pack, making New York the most expensive place in the United States to buy a pack of cigarettes.

So what were smokers in New York to do? They certainly wouldn't all quit smoking. They would just have to buy cigarettes outside New York. Since more than 78 percent of New Yorkers don't own cars, the Internet became the perfect medium to distribute cheaper cigarettes, and 15 million packs sold online in the first month after the tax was enacted. According to Rebecca Lieb in an August 2002 article for *ClickzZ,* "In only four weeks, over $100 million was redirected from the cash registers of delis and newsstands to Indian reservations and other out-of-state vendors."

Before you try to sell your product online, ask yourself if your customers need to buy it online.

E-tailers saw a need and acted. And the cigarette industry is not the only industry booming online. Overall online consumer sales jumped 26 percent from July 2001 to July 2002, by which time they were averaging $6 billion US per month.

"This is one of the only US economic sectors experiencing double-digit growth this year," wrote Lieb. "It's because buying online increasingly fits consumer needs . . . Look at what's growing: travel, computer hardware, and, most of all, financial services and information. All offer solid incentives to buy online."

What Sells and What Doesn't Sell Online

Unfortunately, marketing and sales success do not always go together. An example of a company that was very successful at marketing itself online but unsuccessful at selling products online was Petopia (see Case Study). Besides pet supplies, other items that are difficult to sell online are designer clothing and large items such as furniture and appliances (the main reason <www.Furniture.com> failed). Besides the high cost of shipping heavy items, the chief deterrent to such online sales is that customers want to be able to touch a product before deciding to make an expensive purchase.

CASE STUDY

Petopia launched a million-dollar ad campaign to sell pet products online. But no matter how big their online marketing efforts were, their product was not right for the web. They never created a "need" for buying pet supplies online. Shipping costs were a primary factor affecting Petopia's online sales. People just didn't want to pay high shipping costs for a heavy bag of discount cat litter or dog food when they could buy the same product at almost any grocery store. Plus, most additional purchases people make for their pets are impulse buys, like cute chew toys and treats.

Petopia closed its online store in February 2001 and its domain name now points to <www.Petco.com>, one of its initial investors. Petco now uses the website to help promote its 500-plus retail stores. The website sells pet products online, but also provides a community for pet owners, as well as articles and health information about pets. However, the site's primary function is to promote Petco's retail stores and their overall brand as pet experts, not generate online sales.

A study by Forrester Research and the National Retail Federation found that US Internet users feel more comfortable spending money on small-ticket items, the most popular categories being software, music, books, toys, small appliances, gardening supplies, and flowers — basically, anything consumers don't feel the need to touch.

This information applies especially to small businesses. Online stores tied to an established retail chain are much more likely to find success in selling big-ticket items than small, home-based businesses. This is because consumers are already familiar with the quality and "feel" of products from recognized brands.

Let's take expensive clothing for an example. Banana Republic recently moved its specialty sizes (petites and longs) out of its brick-and-mortar stores and into its virtual store, <www.BananaRepublic.com>. Typically, I would never pay $400 for a suit that I had not tried on first, but I will buy from BananaRepublic.com for a couple of reasons. One, I have been inside their stores, touched their clothing, and know how their sizes fit. The second reason is that there are two Banana Republic stores less than ten miles from where I live, making it very convenient to return items that don't fit quite right. The final, most important reason why I would buy a $400 suit that I had never touched or tried on is that the marketing folks at Banana Republic created a genuine need for me to shop online, just like the New York tobacco tax did. Because I am above average height, I need extra-long pants. Long sizes from Banana Republic are available only online.

Setting Your Online Goals

Okay, so let's assume that you are not Banana Republic. You are a small business trying to promote, sell, and brand your company online. You have committed to providing consistent customer service and have established that there is a genuine need for your product or service. The final step is to determine your overall business goal and make sure that it is in fact something that can be accomplished online.

Before I ever start a marketing campaign for a small-business client, I ask them, "What are your primary goals in having a website?" Most people will answer this question quickly with a comment like, "To sell my services!" or "To promote my product, of course!" It is important to take those answers a step further and determine exactly how you plan to sell your service or promote your product.

If your primary goal of having a website is to sell a product or service, determine how you want to close the sale. Do you want your customers to buy online? Do you want them to pick up the phone and make an appointment? Maybe you want them to come into your office or storefront. Determine exactly what action you want your customers to take when they visit your website and make sure every page encourages them to take that action. Because you are a small business, your marketing efforts must be very precise and targeted. General marketing promoting multiple actions is expensive.

Even if you don't sell your product online, you can still use the web to generate offline sales.

But what if your product is pet food or expensive artwork? Just because people may not buy your product online doesn't mean you shouldn't use the Internet to market it. The Pepsi-Cola case study exemplifies everything that online marketing is supposed to be. It shows a complete synergy between the brand, offline sales, customer communications, and effective co-branding efforts.

More and more often, effective online campaigns significantly help offline sales. A recent study by DoubleClick and Information Resources found that online advertising markedly influences consumer perceptions of an offline brand in a positive way. In the case of major consumer packaged goods, offline sales were increased by an average of 6.6 percent by online ads.

CASE STUDY

When Pepsi-Cola launched its website <www.PepsiStuff.com> in 2000, the site became the centerpiece of one of the most successful advertising campaigns in Pepsi's 103-year history — and the company didn't sell a single bottle or can of Pepsi online.

According to John Gaffney's article in Business 2.0, here's how it worked: Pepsi printed special codes underneath more than 1.5 billion caps of plastic Pepsi bottles. Each code was worth 100 points, which could be used to shop online for prizes such as clothing and CDs.

Taking the campaign online had its advantages from the very beginning. Right away, Pepsi-Cola saved more than $10 million US simply by not having to print prize catalogs. Pepsi also benefited from its partnership with Yahoo! (See chapter 7 for more information about online co-branding opportunities.) With Yahoo! hosting and providing technical assistance to the PepsiStuff.com website, Pepsi was able to sidestep having to manage its own high-traffic e-commerce site. In exchange for its technical assistance, Yahoo! received co-branding on all PepsiStuff bottles and in-store displays, as well as $5 million US in television and print exposure.

During the online campaign, overall national sales of single-serve Pepsi bottles jumped 5 percent. That is a huge accomplishment considering that overall soda sales increased by only 0.2 percent the previous year. More important, the online campaign allowed Pepsi to collect 3.5 million customer profiles, which included golden demographic information such as customer name, e-mail address, zip code, and date of birth. Once Pepsi's marketing team could confirm who their target audience was, they were able to create additional extremely effective marketing campaigns both online and offline.

Demographic information collected during the PepsiStuff campaign solidified the company's decision to place Britney Spears in its Super Bowl commercial. The Britney Spears campaign proved to be a huge success with Pepsi's target audience. In only nine days, more than 1.1 million people logged on to <www.Yahoo.com> and downloaded the television commercial. For consumers to actively take the time to download a commercial shows that Pepsi appealed to its target audience with overwhelming success.

Stats to Support Online Marketing

In 2002, the US government released a report stating that 54 percent of Americans use the Internet on a regular basis. One-third of those people are using the Internet to search for specific product or service information. More than half of the US Internet users will purchase goods and services online. Unlike a couple of years ago, when hundreds of online stores closed daily during the dot.com fallout, today consumers see online stores as more stable. Print, radio, and TV are no longer the only media available to generate trust in your online brand.

A 2001 study by Edison Media Research and Arbitron found that one-third of Americans with home Internet access would give up TV if forced to choose between the tube and the web. Not surprisingly, the people most likely to give up TV were younger — the consumers of the future. Forty-seven percent of people now aged 12 to 24 said they'd rather have the Internet than TV if they had to choose.

When you combine all those stats, the bottom line is that if you are not using the Internet to market your product, you are missing out on a competitive advantage and wasting money at the same time. The wonderful thing about online marketing is that any size business can create an online campaign like Pepsi's even on the smallest budget. In the upcoming chapters, you'll learn how to create campaigns like the big guys' and turn your website into a powerful marketing tool for your products and services.

CHAPTER 2

ATTRACTING YOUR TARGET AUDIENCE

The key to making your online business a success is knowing and identifying with your target audience. When clients come to me for advice on how to drive more customers to their website, the first thing I have them do is list the characteristics of their ideal customers.

What Are the Characteristics of Your Ideal Customer?

You can figure out what type of customer you are trying to target by answering some of the following questions:

▶ What age group are you targeting?

▶ Are you targeting a specific gender or ethnic group?

▶ What is your target audience's average household income?

▶ How computer literate is your target audience?

- Will your customers be more likely to access your website from home or from work?

- How fast is your customers' Internet connection likely to be?

- Does your target audience have any special hobbies?

- In what part of the country are your customers most likely to live?

- Are your customers single or married?

- Do your customers have children?

- What is the education level of your target audience?

To effectively target your ideal audience, you must first understand who your audience is.

Knowing some basic characteristics about your customer will help you determine the most effective marketing plan and design the most appealing website. Appropriate design and content will dramatically increase your success in delivering a clear, innovative message to a highly targeted audience.

The number-one advantage of marketing online is that the Internet allows you to get extremely targeted, more so than any other form of advertising. So the more you know about your customers, the better your chances of a successful campaign. If you don't know who your target audience is, start asking! Give away a product or coupon to encourage your customers to share their demographics.

How to Target Different Types of Audiences

Effective online marketing is no different than marketing cars, music, clothing, or anything else. Certain basic themes, lingo, technology, and even colors appeal to one generation, gender, or race more than another. So get to know your audience, cater to their individual needs; and remember, not all web users are created alike.

By utilizing features that attract specific audiences to a website, you will be able to capture their trust, attention, and loyalty. Here are three examples of very different audiences: women, seniors, and teens.

Women want to save time and money

According to WomenTrend, a Washington consulting firm, 80 percent of all household purchases are made or influenced by women. In 2000, 52 percent of online shoppers were women. The likelihood of web use among women tends to increase with age. CommerceNet/Nielsen Media Research says that women older than the age of 50 are more likely than men to purchase online and twice as likely to purchase as are women in general.

Women of all ages primarily use the Internet to save time and money. They see the value in 24-hour availability and being able to compare prices quickly and easily without any sales pressure — which could be one reason car and financial sites are now thriving!

Women also enjoy a sense of community, which helps explain why <www.women.com> and <www.iVillage.com> are so successful. These sites not only give women a sense of community and comfort, but also help women with everyday-life problems. The number of women who visit education, health, and family sites is drastically higher than the number of men. To sum up, if you are trying to target women, be sure your site provides some of those features that interest them.

Seniors prefer simple sites

Although younger users may seem to be dominating the web now, seniors are gaining ground. Web users aged 55 to 64 make up 22 percent of online households and are estimated to account for 40 percent as more of the baby boomers reach retirement, according to Forrester Research.

With household incomes averaging about $60,000, seniors are an attractive target for online businesses. Although they are more skeptical about the security issues of buying online than younger web users, they are quickly becoming more confident about making web purchases. Just be sure to always provide contact information, including a physical address and phone number. Most seniors agree that they will not buy from a website that does not provide this important information up front. For them, hidden contact information is a big red flag.

Overall, what kind of sites do seniors like best? Simple ones, with light graphics and no complicated downloads or plug-ins.

Determine who your target audience is, then provide website content and features that will keep them interested.

Teens represent a large, racially diverse generation

You better get to know this group. "Think of them as the quiet little group about to change everything," says Edward Winter of The U30 Group consulting firm.

Generation Y is larger than any other consumer group. After all, they are the children of the baby boomers. This generation is also the most racially diverse. According to *Business Week* ("Cover Story: Generation Y"): "One in three is not Caucasian. One in four lives in a single-parent household. Three in four have working mothers."

For this 18 and younger crowd, the web is where it's at. Traditional advertising tactics just won't cut it anymore. This group is far too sophisticated and computer savvy. Says *Business Week*, "[The Internet] is the Gen Y medium of choice, just as network TV was for boomers. Television drives homogeneity, the Internet drives diversity." They find what to wear, what to buy, and what to listen to from two main sources: their peers and online. A well-designed website is crucial for any company hoping to reach this generation, perhaps the most computer literate yet. BMW is a perfect example of a company that zeroed in on their target audience and created an online promotion that attracted their ideal customers while strengthening their overall brand.

CASE STUDY

"We knew that 85 percent of the people who buy our cars are web savvy," said BMW's Marketing vice president, Jim McDowell, during an interview with John Gaffney for *Business 2.0.* "Our buyers are fast-track people who usually have success early in their careers. They believe that the Internet is a wonderful thing."

With this in mind, the company launched the BMW Films campaign, a brilliant way to ensure BMW kept its cutting-edge and high-end brand in the forefront of its equally sophisticated and hip customers. There was nothing low-budget about this campaign, as BMW enticed big-name directors (such as Ang Lee, John Frankenheimer, and Guy Ritchie) and stars (such as Forest Whitaker, Mickey Rourke, and Madonna) to create six- to eight-minute films that provided the elusive mix of entertainment and product showcasing.

Log on to <www.BMWfilms.com>, and if you are truly BMW's target audience (that is, a hip, wealthy, Internet-savvy car lover with a sound card and fast Internet connection), you can download Guy Ritchie's short film featuring Madonna in the back seat of the newest, coolest BMW being chauffeured at top speed through busy city streets. Or click over to an Ang Lee film, created soon after he completed *Crouching Tiger, Hidden Dragon*, and watch the bad guys chase a mysterious BMW driver (Clive Owen), who is escorting a young Tibetan lama to safety.

Although BMW would not disclose the exact amount spent on the campaign, it did announce that if one million online viewers logged on, the campaign would be a success. They were thrilled to learn that well over three million visitors had watched at least one film. And despite a cooling economy, BMW witnessed its highest car sales during the online campaign, exceeding the 40,000-vehicle mark.

Get the Word Out through Those You Know

Using new technology or doing something truly innovative online will almost always get attention. You don't need top directors and famous faces to make a campaign like BMW films work for your small business or company. Just follow the same formula. For example, a really great Flash movie, photo, animation, or even urban legend can start a buzz about your product or company. Think about the types of e-mails that get forwarded around the world and back — all those silly pictures, jokes, and funny movie clips. Imagine tying in some kind of marketing message and watching your friends, family, co-workers, and neighbors forward the message out to their e-mail lists.

An amazing graphic artist I used to work with created a clever animation with his new company logo and contact information discreetly located at the bottom. He forwarded the cute cartoon to his friends and family hoping they would find the animation clever enough to forward on to their e-mail lists. It worked! His animation quickly spread around the Internet, and when it eventually reached people who were in need of graphic design, they were able to trace the animation back to its owner and give him a call.

Any time you can get word of mouth or get friends to e-mail each other about your website, product, or service, the results are invaluable. Efficient, low-cost online marketing is about quality, not quantity. That's why I am firmly against any sort of e-mail spam or purchasing of e-mail lists. Build your own e-mail list with people who are actually interested in you and your product. (See chapter 5 for ideas on how to build your e-mail list.) And always give people a way to unsubscribe from your list.

Unlike online marketing theories of five years ago, smart marketing is no longer about how many people are on your e-mail list or how many people come to your website, but about how those people respond to and feel about your website, company, and product. Spam cheapens your company brand and takes away consumer trust in your business.

Use your existing e-mail list, no matter how small, and simply suggest that recipients forward your message to friends and family. Or entice them by a message such as "Give your friends and family 10% off by having them sign up to join our list." These are two quick ways to gain access to a new audience without having to buy a list.

How to Personalize Your Website

What if you have no obvious target audience? What if you are selling a general product like soap, toothpaste, pens, or lightbulbs that honestly appeals to everyone no matter what their sex, age, or income level? Even if your company has something to offer everyone, that doesn't let you off the hook as far as personalizing your website. Unlike television, radio, or print advertising, it is possible for a website to appear personalized, without limiting your audience.

A big-budget company could spend upwards of a million dollars just on the technology alone that goes into creating a personalized website. The continued success of Amazon.com is a direct result of its extremely efficient use of its personalization technology. Everyone likes books and CDs no matter what their demographic profile is. However, Amazon.com has managed to personalize their online store to fit each new shopper almost perfectly. This is what personalization technology is all about.

Learn from Amazon.com

In case you have never purchased a book or CD on Amazon.com, here's a rundown of how their personalization technology works. When you search for a product on <www.Amazon.com>, the website records this, then uses that information to target ads and messages to you.

I recently purchased Madonna's *Music* CD online. At the virtual checkout stand, the website suggested more products related to my purchase and provided a list of CDs purchased by other people who like Madonna. Before my purchase was completed, Amazon.com directed me to one last page encouraging me to send a coupon for my same Madonna CD to my friends and family. This is a great example of viral marketing. Rather than Amazon.com soliciting new customers, the e-mail coupon (and product endorsement) would come directly from me — a trusted family member or friend.

A few weeks after my purchase, I received an e-mail telling me about a new CD. The e-mail said, "Hi Holly. As someone who just purchased Madonna's latest CD, we thought you'd like 10% off these CDs." The message included a list of CDs by artists similar to Madonna, along with direct links for more information about each CD.

Amazon.com goes so far as to customize its home page based on products a customer has purchased recently. Each time I visit Amazon.com from my home computer, the top of the screen says, "Welcome Back, Holly! Here are some recommended products for you . . ." When I visited the home page of Amazon.com recently, it listed a Madonna biography, poster, and other items I might like based on my recent purchase.

Now this is personalization at its best. From tracking a customer's movement and purchase patterns, it comes full circle through follow-up e-mails and a personalized home page. This may be a perfect use of personalization, but it's also a multi-million-dollar technology.

On a limited budget, you won't be able to achieve personalization on the same scale as Amazon.com. However, there are some basic and very effective things you can do with little to no budget that will give your customers the illusion of personalization and ultimately make them think, "This website is for me!"

Organize and customize content

You can effectively personalize your website by organizing its content and making sure the site's focus is on the customer rather than on your organization.

Recently a local travel agency asked me to take a look at their website and give them some feedback about how to increase online travel bookings without having to create a whole new site or implement expensive booking technology. The travel site offered hundreds of packages to various cities all over Mexico. The site navigation was broken down by city.

I suggested that in addition to categorizing their travel packages by city, they also divide resorts and packages into categories such as "Family Resorts," "Romantic Getaways," or "Adventure Travel." After determining a breakdown that made sense, I suggested they could take the categories a step farther by breaking them down by price. For example, "Luxury Family Resorts" and "Economy Family Resorts." By aiming each package at a specific audience, they would help their customer make a confident decision.

When customers have too many choices, they tend to not make a decision at all. This is one of the biggest problems on the Internet: information overload. Organizing information is key. Making information feel as if it is directed to your customer personally is even better.

In addition to reorganizing and naming their travel packages, I suggested they implement a simple site search engine, so customers can quickly find the exact resorts or condos they are looking for. If you have more than 25 products, a simple search engine is a great feature. It will add to the professionalism and utility of your website without you having to spend money on expensive technology. (See chapter 11 for more information on cost-effectively working with your web developer.)

Online marketing shouldn't stop once a sale is made. The best way to generate new customers is through your existing customer base (just as Amazon.com did when they suggested I e-mail my friends and family a coupon). I suggested that the travel agency give their clients a spot on their website to post photos from their trip. This will not only serve as a genuine customer testimonial, but also encourage that customer's friends and family to visit the site — and, with any luck, book their own trip. Implementing viral marketing concepts and tools such as "Send a postcard," "E-mail my trip itinerary," or "Tell a friend" are great ways to generate quality leads.

Focus on the customer

Another company, called Activation Imaging, wanted their website to generate more sales leads. Their website was nicely designed and professional. It featured standard navy blue colors and stock photos of business executives. Yet although the site looked professional, there was nothing on it that felt personalized. Nothing jumped out and said, "This site is for you!"

I asked them who their top clients were (their target audience), and they quickly listed real estate agencies, biotech companies, and law firms. However, nowhere on their home page did they mention these industries. In fact, all of the text on their home page was about Activation Imaging. Focusing exclusively on self-promotion online is a common mistake of small businesses. Your customer doesn't care about you; they care about what you can do for them. You have ten seconds to capture an Internet user's attention when they visit your home page, so you had better tell that person why they need you. Use your home page to tell your customers why your product or service is right for them, personally. In short, put your company information or personal bio in the "About us" section of your website, not on your home page.

With this in mind, we simply rearranged Activation Imaging's home page to include three boxes. One had a picture of a lawyer, the next a real estate agent, and the last a biotech student. Each image had a sentence appealing to that target audience, followed by "Click here for more info." We then developed an entire page dedicated to why Activation Imaging was an expert in creating digital documents for that specific industry. In reality, we only had to change a few sentences on each page, because the company performs essentially the same service for each industry, but the targeted new sentences now made their product appear personalized.

Testing Your Website's Appeal to Your Target Audience

How can you be sure that your website is attracting the right audience? Just ask them. Although Internet users are getting more and more protective of their personal information, if you offer something of value, they will provide you with this information.

Free products, coupons, and contests are great ways to get the demographic information you need. Emphasize the fact that visitors can trust your company by putting a privacy policy in a prominent place on your website, stating that you will not share their personal information with outside parties and vendors. And, most important, adhere to this policy. Getting your customers' private demographic information is the same as getting their trust. Don't abuse their trust by selling their information.

Knowing the demographics of your customer will help you better spend your marketing dollars and get the most out of your online promotions. A few years ago, market share was king. Today, the success of a website is determined by the quality of the traffic, not the quantity. The key to a successful website and online marketing strategy is being as targeted as possible, even if that leaves you with a smaller audience.

Banner Ads Rely on Placement

When we first launched our Baja travel website, we wanted to buy some banner ads on Yahoo! After all, at the time, Yahoo! was the most popular site on the Internet. We pulled together our meager budget and purchased about 100,000 impressions on the main Yahoo! Travel page. We sat back and waited for the traffic to come rolling in. The result was more than disappointing. We made the number one mistake most first-time online marketers make; we tried to reach the greatest amount of people, rather than a few of the right people. First of all, our 100,000 impressions were completed in a matter of hours and we got a 0.02 percent click-through rate. And of the 0.02 percent people who visited our website, not one person purchased anything. The campaign was a complete waste of marketing dollars. We knew we had to rethink our strategy — fast.

First off, I do not recommend buying banner ads, especially if you are on a limited budget. Banner ads can be effective at branding your company — if you have a large enough budget, negotiate some long-term contracts with prominent websites in your industry — but the actual click-through results are often so low that they are not cost-effective.

If you do choose to buy banner ads, the most cost-effective strategy is to buy them on a very targeted page. The more targeted the page, the cheaper the ad, and the more results you will get. Take our Baja website, for example. Rather than buying a banner ad on Yahoo!'s main Travel page, we should have dug deeper into the Yahoo! Travel site and looked up Mexico, then Baja, then determined which sites were already ranked number one on Yahoo! or were partners with Yahoo! Travel services.

We later went ahead and purchased banners on those sites, at a fraction of the cost of banners on the main Yahoo! Travel page. These sites did not get as much traffic as Yahoo! Travel, but the traffic they did get was more likely to click on our banner ad and purchase our products. These banner ads proved much more successful for us. The banners were cheaper, and the click-through rate averaged 4 percent, which is higher than the industry standard rate of 2 percent.

Another example of targeting your banner ad placement is embedding it in content. Before you buy an ad, ask the website editors what types of stories or promotions they may be doing that would relate to your business, then ask for ads on those pages. If the site has a keyword search, ask to have your banners come up when words associated with your primary product or service are entered.

The deeper the page in the site, the better, because you will be reaching visitors who are truly searching for your information. This strategy is directly aimed at those companies looking to get the most value for their online marketing dollar. For companies with a larger budget, I would recommend buying banners on the home pages for branding purposes. However, branding is expensive, with the average cost of establishing a dominant online brand estimated at US$80 million. So for the purpose of online marketing on a shoestring budget, don't waste your time or money on home page banner ads. (For more on banner ads, see chapter 9.)

Specific Keywords Work Best

Perhaps the most effective way to spend your online budget is buying keywords. Log on to <www.Overture.com> (formerly <www.GoTo.com>) to find out the price of keywords in your industry. Remember, the more specific and targeted your words are, the better. Before you buy your keywords, remember your primary goal and buy keywords that encourage visitors to take that action. The more general the word, the more expensive, and the less likely you will be to generate a customer.

When my friend Sandra got her real estate license in San Diego last year, she wanted to use online marketing to promote her property listings. She was having trouble getting traffic to her new website, so she asked me for advice. "First," I told her, "put yourself in the shoes of the customer. What words would they use on Yahoo! or AOL to find your service?"

Sandra logged on to Overture.com to purchase the keyword term "real estate agents." Ouch! The keyword cost $1.20. That might not sound like much, but when you multiply $1.20 by the more than 50,000 people who searched for that phrase on the Overture.com website alone, that would have set her back a big chunk of cash. Sure, such a general phrase would have generated a great amount of traffic, but was a businessperson looking for commercial property in New Jersey really who Sandra was trying to target? No.

So she tried again, this time with a more targeted focus. She tried "San Diego homes for sale." The price was getting better, at $0.85 per click-through. But the search rate being 1,865 searches per month would have put the price at $15,000 per month. Still way too expensive. One more time. She tried "San Diego beach homes for sale." Bingo! Only five cents. She then went on to purchase the following words as well:

- San Diego beach homes ($0.05)
- 2 bedroom homes in San Diego ($0.05)
- San Diego condos for sale ($0.08)
- San Diego condos ($0.20)

Her most expensive purchase ended up being "San Diego real estate agent," for $0.62 a click-through.

The keyword phrases Sandra purchased were very targeted. They won't get as many searches as "real estate agents," but the people who do search "San Diego beach homes" will click through to her website and are most likely to give her a call.

I talk more about keyword purchases and how to determine a monthly budget level that is right for your business in chapter 8. But before you start buying keywords, let's take a look at your current website. The next chapter includes information on how to create effective web content that will make those keyword purchases even more effective and keep your customers coming back for more.

Use Worksheet 1 to help you determine who your target audience really is.

Worksheet 1
DISCOVERING YOUR TARGET AUDIENCE

Chapter 2 examined the importance of defining your target audience before starting an on-line marketing campaign. Think about the following demographics, and check off the ones that apply to your product or service. In some cases, the answer may be "all of the above." However, remember that general marketing is expensive. The more specific you can be about whom you are trying to reach, the cheaper and more cost-effective your online marketing campaign will be.

Gender

Male ❑

Female ❑

Age Group

Under 18 ❑

18–25 ❑

25–30 ❑

30–35 ❑

35–40 ❑

40–50 ❑

50–60 ❑

60 plus ❑

Annual Household Income Level

Less than $25,000 ❑

$26,000–$35,000 ❑

$36,000–$50,000 ❑

$51,000–$70,000 ❑

$71,000–$99,000 ❑

$100,000–$200,000 ❑

More than $200,000 ❑

Education Level

High school ❑

Bachelor's Degree ❑

Graduate Degree ❑

Marital Status

Married ❑

Single ❑

Divorced ❑

Children? Yes ❑ No ❑

Possible Occupations: _____

(professional, administrative, labor)

Geographic Location: _____

(specific cities, states, regions, or countries)

Ethnicity: _____

(Caucasian, Hispanic, Asian, etc.)

What type of Internet user is your target customer?

Novice ❑

Intermediate ❑

Advanced ❑

Where will your target customers use a computer?

Home ❑

Office ❑

Other ❑

Worksheet 1 — Continued

What types of hobbies do they have? *(E.g., fishing, camping, traveling)*

_____

_____

Other important characteristics your ideal customer would have:

_____

_____

Now, list at least ten websites below that you think the above customer would visit. These are the types of websites you should want to buy ads on, form partnerships with, or emulate in content and design.

1. _____

2. _____

3. _____

4. _____

5. _____

6. _____

7. _____

8. _____

9. _____

10. _____

CHAPTER 3
CREATE EFFECTIVE CONTENT

Leave static information to print. The web is meant to be flexible and always changing. If a customer doesn't feel a website is "alive" with fresh content, promotions, and ideas, he or she can only assume it is "dead" — abandoned, with no customer service behind it. Your home page is the most important piece of your online marketing campaign. The stories, images, and information on your home page create your overall company brand. The more professional and useful this information, the more credible your product or service becomes to the user.

Survey Demonstrates Importance of the Web

According to a 2002 survey conducted by Nielsen/NetRatings and the *Washington Post* (reported by Internet News), 77 percent of key business decision makers believe that the Internet is the absolute best place to find out about new products. That ranks the Net higher than magazines, newspapers, radio, and even television. By using the web to market your product, you have the opportunity to put your product in front of the most demographically desirable customers during the web's prime time, the business day.

Carolyn Clark, Internet media analyst at Nielsen/NetRatings, said, "The web, and particularly online news, has established itself as a powerful medium for reaching and influencing business decision makers. Not only are business decision makers spending more time on the Internet when compared to other media, more than 60 percent recommend online advertising as a key marketing vehicle to reach them."

Online Publishers Association executive director Michael Zimbalist, in the same article, said, "The findings of the washingtonpost.com study provide further proof that online advertising is the best way for smart marketers to reach the most influential audiences. Their usage is concentrated during the daytime, while they are at work, and undistracted by other media choices."

The study found that the Internet is not only the most used medium during the workday, but also more than 90 percent of executives who use the Internet regularly at work log on from home as well. This makes the Internet's audience during after-business hours second only to television. The more educated the user and the higher the household income, the higher the number of web users to TV viewers.

Key Components of Great Web Content

So what does this information have to do with your website's content? Well, whether it's early Monday morning over a cup of steaming java at the office or late Friday night with a couple of friends, Internet users are looking for one or more of the following:

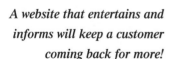

A website that entertains and informs will keep a customer coming back for more!

- ◗ Entertainment
- ◗ Information
- ◗ Community

Provide at least one of these key ingredients, and your website is on its way to attracting some loyal customers.

REI.com, a consumer cooperative that supplies specialty outdoor gear, is a perfect example of a website that effectively combines all three of these key ingredients to create an enormously successful web presence. Autobytel.com is another website whose complete content and interactive information create an overall trusted resource that translates into solid sales for the company. (See the two case studies.)

Creating a website of truly valuable content not only gives your site credibility, but also positions your company as an industry expert in your customer's eyes. But maintaining the more than 45,000 content pages and 75,000 products on the REI website or updating the hundreds of new car features on the Autobytel.com site is no easy task. Both companies employ hundreds of people in their Internet departments alone, just to keep up with the enormous amount of website content.

Sound like a lot of work to keep your website looking fresh? It doesn't have to be. Fortunately, small businesses can take advantage of some time-saving and cost-efficient ways to keep their site updated without employing hundreds of content developers.

CASE STUDY

With a conversion rate of a whopping 10 percent of all visits, REI.com generates more sales than any one of its brick-and-mortar stores. By combining expert product information with a sense of community, REI keeps a strong hold on its reputation as a leader in the outdoor adventure industry. The company uses its own customers to generate a good portion of the site's content through the "Learn and Share" section. Here, visitors interact by posting questions, advice, and stories on the REI message board, which further promotes the REI-brand lifestyle.

The vast message boards are organized into two main sections, "Learn" and "Share." In the "Learn" section, anglers, hikers, rock climbers, snowboarders, and outdoor adventurers can find helpful tips and advice about their favorite sports. The right side of the page includes REI products that complement each tip. The "Share" section gives these same outdoor recreationists a chance to meet others just like them to plan trips, share experiences, or talk about their favorite REI products.

Each quarter, REI does a great job of creating a seasonal feel through the colors and graphics on their home page. The minute you log on to REI.com, you instantly get in the mood to purchase that new snowboard for winter, water skis for summer, camping gear for spring, or new clothing for fall. The catalog site doubles as an online adventure magazine, giving advice and stories on the best places to travel and use new REI products. Visitors can even go so far as to book a REI Adventures trip through the site. With so much well-organized content to choose from, the outdoor adventurer can't help but keep on clicking.

CASE STUDY

Autobytel.com provides all the information car shoppers need about their favorite cars, from safety features to price quotes, insurance information, and financing warranties. It even takes them on a virtual tour inside the car — all without the sales pressure of a dealer.

Women are a huge target for this type of service, because they despise the pressure of hard sales. Women like to be able to research and get the information they need fast, in a no-pressure environment. Autobytel took this important audience into consideration when they created the "Autobytel.com for Her" section. This section focuses on vehicle safety records and manufacturer recalls as well as automobile reviews written by women.

And the Autobytel network doesn't stop with the final sale. Users can log onto the "My Garage" section and get important updates on things such as recall information, real-time service reminders, repair cost estimates, and even do-it-yourself tips.

Low-Cost Ways to Generate Fresh Content

One of the most common ways businesses keep their web pages looking new without employing round-the-clock staff is by designing five to ten different home pages and then switching them around each month. Spend a week or two coming up with different home page ideas. You can create random home page promotions with timeless messages and images or make them more seasonal by planning a "Holiday Special" or "Back to School" sale.

Coming up with different home page features all at once will not only force you to plan out your marketing efforts for the year, but, more important, it will save you time in the long run, as you won't have to think about your website content again for at least 12 months. Ask your web developer to put these new home pages on a timer or rotating script. The home pages can be set up to automatically rotate to showcase a new coupon, tip of the month, or featured product as often as you want.

When I worked on the Jenny Craig website, we uploaded five to seven weight loss success stories to a rotating script on the home page every month. Each time a visitor logged on to <www.JennyCraig.com>, they were greeted with a new face and a new success story. It was a very effective, low-energy way to keep the site changing daily.

Think of your home page as being like a magazine cover. You wouldn't subscribe to a magazine that had the same photo and copy on the cover every month. So why would you keep your home page the same month after month? And just like a magazine cover, you wouldn't feature all of your content on the home page; your readers would be overwhelmed! It's much more effective to choose one or two key features or products to showcase. The rest of your products and information should be organized within the appropriate pages of your site. When it's time to update your home page, simply pull content from these other pages. This way, you don't have to create any new content, just reorganize it so it looks new to the visitor.

Dangers of Changing Your Home Page Too Much

Although you want your website to stay looking fresh, you're only asking for trouble if you change it too much. Web users look for comfort in their favorite sites, and comfort comes from familiarity. You run the risk of confusing visitors and could also compromise your search engine positioning if your website doesn't maintain a core consistency.

Visitors could become confused

The most important thing to remember when updating your home page with new content is not to confuse your visitors. Changing a story or graphic on your home page shouldn't change the whole look and feel of your site. Customers should be able to easily find the same information they always have. The navigation tools and section headers should never change.

Think about it: how do you feel when your favorite website that you log on to every Monday morning to get your stock quotes or weather or news gets a whole new redesign? You get confused and frustrated! Be consistent with your main navigation and site features. Swap images and stories for similar images or stories. You want your site to appear fresh without appearing like a totally different site.

For example, although the JennyCraig.com site was different every day, it wasn't confusing to the user because we were swapping similar images and stories. The success stories all had the same feel, with similar information and purpose. Don't take out your customer log-in graphic and substitute it with a press release or update your job openings section with a new product section. This just gets confusing.

Every time I log on to the Bank of America website, I know exactly where to log in to check my account and exactly where to look for banking advice or promotions. Even though they are constantly featuring new graphics or promotions on the home page, it is not confusing to me because the core navigation, colors, and themes are consistent. There is certain comfort to a website that is always consistent. If you can depend on a website to consistently provide you with the information you expect, then you're likely to anticipate consistent quality service as well. For small businesses, gaining a customer's trust (and therefore business) is often synonymous with perceived dependability and consistency.

You could hurt your search engine position

Making drastic changes to your home page content can also be detrimental to your search engine positioning. Some search engines "spider" sites anywhere from three weeks to three months from submission. Without going into too much detail here (you'll find more on search engine positioning in chapter 8), search engines look at every piece of your web page from home page text to ALT tags in your graphics, and the longer that certain keywords stay consistent, the higher your site will be ranked. Search engines don't want to feel that they were "tricked" into indexing your site for one thing, then have your content change to reflect something else.

To avoid this common problem, walk a fine line between keeping things similar and keeping things looking new. The best way to accomplish this is to keep the majority of your home page the same and change only a fraction of it. That way, visitors will still get fresh content but you won't have to worry about your site dropping off the charts.

Benefits of a Flexible Home Page

Once you and your web developer have mastered the art of keeping your home page updated while not changing the core content of your site, you are on your way to experiencing the valuable benefits of a flexible home page.

Test campaigns and track successes

Having a flexible home page gives your business a testing ground for all of your offline marketing efforts. Before you sink your hard-earned dollars into a newspaper or magazine ad, test it out on your website. See how users react. You can easily use your home page to find out which featured products or coupons attract the most sales or maybe which image generates the most interest in your company.

To obtain this type of information, you will need access to web tracking software. Through web tracking software, you can get detailed market data that isn't possible from any other type of medium. You will be able to see which images your customer clicked on and what page they were on when they left your website. NetTracker, Urchin, LiveStats, and Web Trends are all good programs for tracking a customer's movement through your website. Ask your web developer or hosting company which one they use, because most programs available today offer similar features. Getting access to a web tracking program is most often just a simple upgrade to your existing hosting package.

Keep focused on your target audience

Great content doesn't just refer to enticing promotions, stories, or graphics. It refers to anything on your website that encourages positive communication, reaction, and interaction with your target audience while delivering them important information about your product, company, service, or beliefs. Great content can include message boards, chatrooms, video clips, Flash movies, or anything else that makes your customer excited about your website and product.

However, be sure your content is relevant and appeals to your target audience. For example, you don't want a disruptive musical promotion if your most common customer is an executive logging on from work. And you don't want a large video download if your customer is most likely dialing up from a home computer. Knowing your target audience (discussed in chapter 2) is the key to generating the most results from your website content.

Ways to Generate Content If You Don't Write

What if you have absolutely no writing or photography skills to create your own content? Should you buy content? Yes and no.

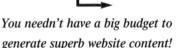

Buy content

I recommend buying images because at the time this book was written you can still find very inexpensive, high-quality web images for about $29.95 on sites such as gettyimages.com. Spending a couple hundred dollars to get a few great images is always worth it. Professional images can make all the difference in giving your website a professional feel. Log on to one of these sites and simply search by feeling, object, season, or anything else you can imagine that might help express your brand image.

I do not recommend buying written content. Although there are many services out there that will feed you content for your website, it is simply not cost-effective for small businesses to buy such a service. Many of these services are aimed at large companies with a huge Internet staff, such as REI or Autobytel. Even if you subscribed to one of these content providers, you would still have to spend the time to choose which stories were appropriate for your website, then make the effort to post them on your site. The goal of using content is to make your website/product/company appear credible, but it takes only a couple of well-placed, timeless stories to make this work. No one expects a small-business site to be the hub of all information related to your industry.

Have customers generate content

That said, how do you generate good content without buying it? One good idea is to take the REI example and have your customers generate some content for you. Create a Frequently Asked Questions section where customers can ask you questions about your product and you can post the answers. This type of information is timeless and can be rotated as a featured question of the week or month.

Another idea is to have a contest. Entice your customers with a special prize or coupon to send you stories about how they used your product or how your service helped them in some way. Then take the best stories and post them on your website. This material doubles as interesting content and a testimonial to your great service. For instance, Zucca Mountain Vineyards <www.zuccawines.com> holds a recipe contest on their website. Customers submit favorite recipes they use to accompany Zucca wine in an effort to win two free bottles. Zucca Mountain Vineyards not only generates some great content for their site, but collects more demographic information on their customers as well.

Link to other sources of content

Another way to provide updated content without writing it yourself is to simply find relevant news headlines, post them on your site, then link to the original story. When 9/11 happened, my husband and I were still running our Mexican travel website. We didn't have the staff power — or the authority for that matter — to get the latest status on the border crossing each day. We knew our customers would be looking to our website for this important information, so we simply posted headlines of the reports and then linked directly to the San Diego Union Tribune, CNN, or whatever news source website was providing information on border security and travel alerts. Our customers didn't expect us to provide custom reports on this, but they did expect us to inform them on what was happening or how to get the information they needed before they took their trip across the border.

Content, especially for small businesses, is not expected to be original, just useful. Your choice of content should show the customer that you care enough about them to post links to articles on safety information, health issues, or anything else that may relate to your specific product or service. Just be sure to always quote your source, and never copy any articles without asking for permission.

Realistically, most people do not log on to a small-businesses website every day, or even once a month, so be sure to label content as new or post a date next to it. After all, the purpose of updating your site is to let new customers as well as existing ones know that there are real people who care about customer service behind that website.

CHAPTER 4

GENERATE FREE ADVERTISING

In traditional media, one positive sentence in editorial is worth much more than two paid advertisements. The same is true on the Internet. Getting a free link or product mention on another website is an extremely valuable way to gain high-quality leads.

Pinpoint Marketing versus Interruptive Marketing

The key to effective marketing is to be able to put your product in front of potential customers at the exact moment when they are looking for it. A New Jersey marketing agency, New Identities, calls this process pinpoint marketing. Pinpoint marketing is in direct contrast to 90 percent of television and radio ads, which are known as interruptive marketing. Interruptive marketing is not only more expensive, but also wasteful of your marketing dollars, because you are trying to put your product in front of everybody, rather than pinpointing exactly who wants to hear about your product and when.

What is pinpoint marketing?

Picture yourself at the ball game eating a bag of dry-roasted peanuts. You're on your second handful when that familiar red-and-white logo pops up on the big screen advertising an ice-cold Coca-Cola. You immediately track down the next vendor with a basket of ice-cold drinks. This is pinpoint marketing. It is the process of delivering an appropriate message at the right time that produces actual results

In contrast, let's say you are eating those same peanuts at the ball game when an advertisement for Toyota trucks pops up on the same screen. It's a nice ad, but not nearly as effective. This is an example of interruptive marketing. It is not truly targeted because it is not what you are actively looking for. Unlike when people watch TV or listen to the radio, Internet users are actively looking for a solution to a problem. If you can place your product in their path at the right time, you've gained a customer.

Pinpoint marketing can help you gain customers by ensuring that your product is exposed to the right people at the right time.

Day-part marketing

Timing and placement have become so critical to online marketing that companies such as NYTimes.com, Yahoo!, and now AOL are selling ads in "day part," which is something the television industry has always done. For example, AOL's day parts are 6 a.m. to noon and noon to 6 p.m. AOL has also included a late-night component with AOL Music programming from 11 p.m. to 6 a.m, which is the time most home users are downloading music. Being able to specify what time of day certain ads run allows you to target your customers more effectively. For example, McDonald's could run 99-cent cheeseburger banners in the afternoon and switch to an Egg McMuffin banner in the early morning.

But this chapter is not about buying banner ads — or even day-part ads, for that matter — because that type of sophisticated ad technology comes with a hefty price. Small businesses need to focus on ways to generate free publicity. The most solid way of doing that is by combining your marketing message with important content.

Embedding Marketing Messages in Content

Let's take the pharmaceutical industry as an example. If a pharmaceutical company were trying to promote the drug Paxil as an antidepressant, effective pinpoint marketing would be planting stories about symptoms of depression (with information about how Paxil can help) within the health and depression pages of popular health websites such as <www.WebMD.com>. Yes, the company could just buy a banner ad in these sections, but their marketing would be more effective if their product link were embedded in an article. It would look more credible and people would be more likely to pay attention to it than to an "interruptive" pop-up ad.

More people than ever are using the Net to research products before they buy. According to an *Internet Wire* article titled "Guerrilla Marketing in the Internet Age" (August 2002), 25 percent of people who respond to television ads that feature a 1-800 number check for the product online first. This number is expected to rise to 50 percent by 2006. Overall, Internet users are getting more serious about their time spent online. A recent study released by the Pew Internet and American Life Project found that a majority of Internet users are spending less overall time on the web, but the time they do spend online is very deliberate and focused. A majority of Internet users already have their favorite sites bookmarked, and they can find a movie time, stock information, or a sports score in a matter of seconds.

Although the average time spent online has dropped from 90 minutes in 2001 to 83 minutes in 2002, the study showed that the more familiar people get with the Net, the more proactively they spend their time. This can be linked to a 45 percent increase in online purchases, from 40 million in 2000 to 58 million in 2001. The more familiar people become with using the Internet and the dependability of their favorite websites, the more comfortable they are spending money online.

The take-away message from these stats is that people research products before they buy. For people wanting to find a solution to their health problem, buy a new CD, take a vacation, or buy a new car, the percentage looking online for information is dramatically rising. Put your product in their research path.

Establishing Credibility

The main problem most small businesses have with selling online is credibility. With all of the Internet scams out there, people are more skeptical than ever of unfamiliar companies. Small, unknown business can gain credibility on the Net by making their company name and logo familiar to users on multiple Internet channels.

One way to do this is to set up a shopping cart on Yahoo! shopping. The cost is less than US$50 per month and well worth every penny. Besides having access to their shopping-cart technology, your company will be affiliated with a major web property, which gives customers confidence to buy online from you. Once a customer orders from your Yahoo! store, they will get more familiar with your company name and be more likely to buy directly from your website or company the next time around.

How to get your content onto other sites

The second way to build online credibility is content swapping. If you can position an article (think consumer research) with a link to your website on a top web property in your field, your chance of credibility and sales success is even higher.

But how can you get web editors to take notice of your company? In chapter 3, you learned just how valuable web content is to companies of all sizes. And you learned just how expensive content can be to purchase. The result is that most companies are willing to trade a free plug for your website for a good story.

When we were running our Baja travel website, we never paid for content. Instead, we had our advertisers write stories about "What to expect on a whale watching adventure in San Ignacio," with a link at the end saying, "For more information, check out Keith Jones's Whale Watching Adventures." Or we'd post an article called "10 Reasons to Love Baja," with a link to Ann Hazard's newest book about traveling in Baja California. Trading content for links is a win-win situation. The content provider gets free, very targeted advertising for their product or service, while the company posting the story (and link) is able to showcase valuable, informative content from professional sources.

I have gotten the best leads for my web design consulting business through articles I have written for industry magazines, not by buying banner ads. When a potential customer reads your article, you have already established yourself as an expert in that field. By the time the customer clicks over to your website or gives you a call, you have a very hot lead.

Internet users want results fast. They know exactly what they are looking for, so your marketing message better be clear-cut, concise, and appropriate. Think about what type of person will be using the magazine website you select to post your content. For example, studies show that a mother of two who needs a quick dinner recipe will do a quick search, then print out the page. So animated banner ads or even a link to your website may not be the most effective way to get her attention. On the other hand, a clip-out coupon that she could take with her to the store after she prints out the recipe page would be very effective.

In contrast, an IT director searching for new company software at work would most likely research the information online, then click over to his or her favorite message boards to confirm his or her finding with other IT experts. If Comp USA had banner ads throughout the IT director's research journey, he or she would recall that and click over to finalize his or her purchase directly online.

Swapping Advertising

Swapping stories, banner ads, coupons, and links is a great way to introduce your product to new audiences. Maybe you are a house painter. Your audience is most likely looking for more home improvement information, so you could exchange stories and "how to" advice with local carpenters or electricians. You can swap content with anyone in your industry who is not a direct competitor. Having the extra content will give your site credibility, and having articles on other sites will help to position your company as an authority.

Short on time? What about banner-ad swapping services such as Link Exchange and Smart Age? These companies will shoot your banner ads across their entire network of thousands of other small-business sites. All you have to do is post other network members' ads on your website. The upside is that your banner ads will end up on all corners of the Net — sometimes in the most unlikely places. The downside is, some of these websites may not have the same professionalism as your site and could lessen your site brand and credibility in the process. Remember, who you exchange links, content, and banners with reflects directly on your company. In my opinion, it is worth the extra time to work on quality exchanges with a few sites, rather than mass banner-ad exchanges with thousands.

How to Generate Word-of-Mouth, Viral Marketing

Viral marketing is one of the most powerful tools the web can offer for spreading the word about your business.

Word of mouth is the second most popular way people discover new websites. (Search engines are the number-one way.) Word of mouth can be generated by e-mails from your friends or message board posts from strangers. Really effective word of mouth is known as viral marketing and is one of the Internet's biggest success stories.

Viral marketing is the same process whereby those familiar e-mail jokes, urban legends, and images get forwarded around the world. It is about taking advantage of humanity's basic need to be social. A person's social network can consist of a few close friends or hundreds of business associates. No matter how small the social group may start out, effective viral marketing is responsible for turning unheard-of small companies with no marketing budget into rock stars in the online world. Even the biggest names on the Net continue to use viral marketing as their primary marketing tool.

Your small business can set up a similar e-mail marketing strategy without a lot of costs or high technology. If you have a small number of employees, you can simply set up an e-mail signature with a marketing message that will automatically be attached to every company e-mail. You can easily set this up on popular e-mail programs such as Eudora and Outlook Express. Look under the "Options" or "Preferences" tab for a signature option.

Take this idea a step further and have your hosting company or IT department attach a marketing message to all outgoing mail through a process called *mail rerouting*. By more sophisticated mail rerouting, you can not only track the results, but also be assured that every outbound message will have the same look and feel . . . and employees cannot alter that. If your current hosting company does not provide this service, look into Rocketseed and Mailround. These companies provide very sophisticated outgoing mail rerouting services that let you place entire graphic commercials into your outgoing mail.

"The main thrust of the idea is to utilize the thousands of e-mails a company will send out every day to its most important audience (i.e., shareholders, clients, suppliers, journalists, etc.) and to make them consistent and branded," explains Mailround's Eldar Turvey. "These e-mails become a source of viral marketing, since our research shows each e-mail is viewed five times on average. Obviously they are forwarded on, replied to, stored for future use, etc., and the branding is prominent on each occasion."

MSN's Hotmail grew exponentially simply by having customers spread the word for them. For Hotmail, it was simple. Give away free e-mail and have your marketing message attached to every outgoing e-mail.

CASE STUDY

Hotmail's branding message was short and sweet: "Get Free E-mail at Hotmail.com." But the simple message was attached to hundreds of thousands of messages by people who used their web-based e-mail daily. The short message quickly helped the company spread the word and increase its customer base.

Besides Hotmail's smart e-mail branding, the second primary factor that led to Hotmail's huge success was the simple fact that they offered something for free: free e-mail.

Offer something for free

"Free" is the most searched word on the Internet. Everyone wants something for free. Give away something for free and the word will spread like wildfire. Free brings traffic. However, most small businesses can't afford to give away free services or products hoping to generate a sale in the future. However, they can get more creative and offer a free (insert product here) for the first 10 people to buy (insert product here). Even something as simple as free movie tickets or a free meal can get attention. Everyone likes to get something for free.

Can you offer something for free? Doing so can drastically increase traffic on your website.

Utilize message boards and chatrooms

Word of mouth and viral marketing techniques flourish on message boards and chatrooms. This is especially true with the under-25 crowd, because younger users want to discover things on their own. Remember how it felt to be the first one to buy the album of that upcoming band? Or hear about that new movie featuring everyone's favorite actor? The Internet generation hates being overmarketed to, which is why guerrilla marketing tactics work so well.

Electric Artists used message boards and chats as a primary medium for promoting their new client, pop singer Christina Aguilera. The company began chatting up Christina's first album before anyone had even heard of her. The buzz about Christina grew infectious. Their strategy was so successful that teens were lined up outside music stores to be the first to purchase her debut album.

A similar phenomenon took place a couple of months before the low-budget movie *The Blair Witch Project* was released (see Case Study).

Think about the types of e-mails that get forwarded around the world — all of those silly pictures, jokes, urban legends, funny movie clips, great Flash animations, and more. E-mail makes it so simple to share things with your friends, family, and business associates. If you can somehow attach your marketing message to one of these infectious e-mails, you can create a buzz about your product or company. Remember the graphic artist I mentioned in chapter 2 who forwarded a clever animation? One positive result of his e-mail marketing was that when he showed his portfolio to potential clients, many of them already recognized his work, although they weren't quite sure where they had seen it. When a potential customer recognizes a company logo or name, you are more likely to get their trust and close a sale.

Choose a memorable domain name

One final important factor to remember when spreading your company information through word of mouth: choose a memorable domain name. Pick something that is easy to remember, easy to spell, and relates to your product. That way, people can easily tell their friends about it.

Once people find your website, the quality of your site's content should keep them returning — perpetuating word of mouth as your number-one marketing tool.

Internet users of all ages seemed to stumble across old newspaper clippings and stories about the Blair Witch, leading thousands of people to forward the creepy stories, then eventually debate via e-mail, message boards, and chatrooms whether or not the legend was true or not.

The Blair Witch Project's viral marketing was arguably the most successful use of guerrilla marketing the movie industry has ever seen. By the time the US$20,000 movie was released, the low-cost marketing strategies paid off. The instant hit generated more than US$150 million in ticket sales, putting it in direct competition with the multi-million-dollar movies in theaters nationwide. As a result of this phenomenal online marketing approach, for the first time bigger companies started to recognize the power of Internet marketing — for all industries.

CHAPTER 5
E-MAIL MARKETING

Since the growth of the Internet, e-mail marketing has become one of the most cost-effective forms of marketing for companies of all sizes. Whether it's business to business (B2B) or business to consumer (B2C), e-mail marketing drastically extends customer service and increases brand loyalty by keeping your company in the forefront of customers' minds. When done correctly, permission-based e-mail marketing can outperform every other type of online marketing strategy. However, no one piece of a marketing campaign can stand alone. A great e-mail newsletter must have the website to back it up and enough interest to build up your e-mail list in the first place. This chapter will explain how to build your e-mail list, create an effective campaign, test it, and professionally launch it.

Stats to Support E-Mail Marketing

E-mail is the number-one activity of Internet users, which is why e-mail can be such an effective marketing tool. According to the 2002 Yankee Group survey, 72 percent of the US population is on-line. Of that group, 93 percent regularly check e-mail from home,

Take the time to build up your own e-mail list rather than purchasing one. The results will be invaluable.

and 85 percent check e-mail from work. Of these Internet users, most say they would rather receive marketing messages via e-mail than be disturbed at dinnertime with a phone call, and they are more likely to look at the messages in their in-box than any junk mail stuffed in their home mailbox.

Permission-Based versus Spam E-Mail

The key to an effective e-mail marketing campaign is to make it permission-based only. In other words, your customers must "opt in" or choose to be on your e-mail list.

Never buy or rent an e-mail list. Buying or renting a list is the same as spam. No matter what an e-mail-list company may tell you about their subscribers, I guarantee that 99.9 percent of those people did not opt in to having their e-mail addresses and personal information sold.

Sending e-mail to people who did not personally request information from your company is spam, period. Spam cheapens your company brand and takes away consumer trust. Just as with your website traffic, the key is quality of leads, not quantity, so take the time to build your own e-mail list. The results will be invaluable.

Think of e-mail marketing as an extension of customer service. San Diego web design and marketing company Interactivate takes pride in its "TouchPoint" e-mail program, which allows its clients to communicate with customers at each point in the sales process.

"We've had incredible success with many of our clients, such as Ladera Ranch, a master-planned community of 8,100 new homes in Orange County," Interactivate's CEO, Jack Abbot, told SignOnSanDiego.com in a 2002 interview by Kim Peterson. "Members on their [e-mail] list receive updates and information at every step in the process, whether they've just begun to look for a home or are in the throes of purchasing. The results speak for themselves: one in 20 members of the Ladera Ranch e-mail list has purchased a home in the community, and that number continues to increase."

Abbot went on to say, "By giving [customers] what they ask for without abusing their permission, we form the basis for a relationship that is built on respect, evolves over time and results in long-term customer loyalty."

Building Your E-Mail List

Generating a quality e-mail list takes some time, but in the end, you'll have a captive audience that is truly interested in your product. But remember, when a customer offers you their private e-mail address and demographic information, it's the same as getting their trust. Don't abuse it.

If you plan to follow a high standard of respect regarding your client's personal information, let them know. Provide a privacy policy on your website promising not to sell customers' information to any outside parties or vendors. Let them know exactly what type of messages they should expect and how frequently. Also, let them know that they have the option to unsubscribe from your list at any time. This will give customers confidence to register for your list.

If you do a joint promotion or co-branding effort with another website or company, don't exchange e-mail lists. Instead, simply put that company's information in your newsletter. The e-mails should always come directly from you. If it looks like you have sold your customers' valuable information to another company, they will lose trust and unsubscribe from your list and reject any future contact with your company.

When enticing people to join your list, don't ask for too much personal information too fast. You wouldn't ask someone you had just met at a cocktail party for their home address and household income. For a website to require this type of information up front, before gaining mutual respect and trust, is just as offensive. Start by asking for only their e-mail address and name. You can fill in the rest of their information with future marketing efforts and promotions. Be patient. Just as with friendships, it takes time to get a clear picture of who your best customers are and what exactly they want out of your newsletter and website.

If your company appears trustworthy (i.e., not going to sell the customer's information), it is not difficult to gather e-mail addresses. Something as simple as a contest or giveaway ("Enter to win a free [insert your product here]"), a coupon or discount ("Subscribe to our newsletter and get 10% off your next purchase"), or even regular content ("Join our newsletter for weekly tips on using our product") will work.

If you have a storefront, this is a great place to collect e-mail addresses. Place a fishbowl or basket at the front desk with a sign announcing that customers can "Win a free lunch" or "Win a free trip" for dropping in their business card. Office Depot does this. When you walk into one of these office supply stores, there is a large briefcase with hundreds of business cards under a sign that reads "Win this briefcase." I know I have dropped my card in there.

Trade shows and networking events are also great places to collect business cards and e-mail addresses. But don't assume everyone that gives you their business card automatically wants to be on your e-mail list. Spam is a very sensitive issue. My rule of thumb is this: if someone gives me their business card or e-mails me a direct question about my service, it is okay to e-mail them a promotional announcement once, to entice them to join my list. If they don't bite, I don't push it. These people did not truly opt in to my list, so it would be considered spam if I continued e-mailing them.

I had a client who owned a men's clothing store and paid his employees $1 per e-mail address they gathered. A dollar may not sound like much, but for store employees making $8 an hour, an extra couple of dollars an hour can really add up. For the business owner, $1 was a small price to pay for such important customer information.

To entice customers who were reluctant to give up their e-mail addresses, he encouraged them with 20 percent off coupons telling them more coupons would be delivered via e-mail. He also noted the privacy policy and reminded them that they could easily un-subscribe anytime. The result was the collection of thousands of quality e-mails. Once his database was comparable to his traditional mailing list, he got rid of his paper mailing list altogether and began to send his catalogs, coupons, and new product info by e-mail only, saving tens of thousands of dollars in the process.

For our Baja website, we doubled our e-mail list every time there was an important tourist event happening in Baja California, Mexico. Our biggest event of the year was the Bisbee's Black and Blue Marlin Jackpot tournament in Cabo San Lucas. Wealthy anglers from all over the world traveled by yacht to the docks of Cabo San Lucas to compete for more than $1 million in prize money. This was exactly the audience we were targeting: adventurous, active tourists in the high-income bracket.

We provided a live webcast of the event, which gained us instant access to the participants. During the weeklong tournament, we'd send our very attractive promotional hostesses down to the docks with clipboards and free products with our company logo and URL (stickers, water bottles, key chains, and so on) to gather demographic information and e-mail addresses. Most people were more than willing to talk to our lovely marketers, and if they needed a little extra incentive, the free products always closed the deal.

At night, we'd bring our digital cameras to the local hot spots and take digital postcards of tourists. We offered to e-mail the pictures to their friends, family, and co-workers back home. For a $5 fee, we let them fill out a form with a short "hello" message along with their e-mail address, plus the e-mail addresses of all the friends they wanted the postcard sent to. Young men would often pay to have their picture taken with our promotional hostesses, then e-mailed to all of their friends back home for bragging rights. But there were many couples who wanted pictures of just the two of them to send a friendly "hello" to their family back home. Each night, we'd use Adobe Photoshop to put our company logo onto the pictures, then e-mail them out with the message requested by the tourist. At the end of the message, we'd encourage them to visit our site and sign up for our newsletter for more information on "What's happening in Cabo" or "Special travel rates to Cabo."

We'd gather hundreds of e-mail addresses from our prime audience during this weeklong event and saw an exponential increase in web traffic, all generated by word of mouth, postcards, and our physical presence in Cabo. Our trips to Cabo every year reminded us that it is important to combine traditional (offline) marketing tactics with online strategies. Sometimes the best way to find new customers is to meet them in person first. Customers like to know that there are real people behind a website.

Goal-Oriented Marketing

Once you've developed your e-mail list, the next step is to develop your e-mail marketing plan. First, define your business goal (what we did in chapters 1 and 2). What do you hope to achieve through e-mail marketing? More leads? Repeat customers? Make sure those goals are reflected in your overall plan. They will give you a way to track the success of your efforts.

E-Mail Newsletters

If you choose to send an e-mail newsletter, you must offer some type of incentive for users to stay on your list.

Content ideas

An e-mailed newsletter can be an excellent way to promote your company, but the content, length, and frequency of publication must all be carefully considered.

Incentives don't always have to be a coupon or a product give-away. Great content is a very effective incentive as well. Ideas for effective newsletter content include the following:

▶ Customer success stories

▶ Interviews with industry experts

▶ Q&A column

▶ Industry stats or news

▶ Customer feedback

▶ Tips on how to use your product

Don't include company history, company news, or "about us" information in your newsletter unless it is being sent to investors. The truth is, your customers just don't care about what's happening in your company. They just want to know how you can help them. Great content is anything that will interest your customers. And just like your home page, your newsletter has only seconds to capture a customer's attention before it ends up in the trash. Tell readers what you can do for them right away and why they should choose your company.

An e-mailed newsletter can be an excellent way to promote your company, but the content, length, and frequency of publication must all be carefully considered.

Why short is sweet

Keep your newsletters tight, short, and to the point. Short means 1,000 words max and no more than five regular departments.

Besides the fact that most people don't like to read long e-mails, there are two other important reasons to keep your e-mails short.

First, long newsletters with multiple departments will be harder for you to keep updated. This could hamper your ability to send newsletters consistently and provide solid new information. Second, if you provide too much information in the initial e-mail, customers won't click through to your website. If they don't click, you will have no way to track the success of your campaign (unless you are e-mailing a printable coupon or have some other way of offline tracking).

What sets online marketing apart from traditional marketing methods is the ability to track campaigns right down to the image people clicked on to buy your product. If your e-mails don't encourage people to click, you won't be able to track what part of your e-mail campaign is working.

I learned this important tip firsthand when I sent out a very thorough e-mail detailing our whole new line of Guayabera Mexican shirts. The e-mail neatly listed all nine of our new shirts complete with a picture, description, and price. The e-mail generated a disappointing 5 percent click-through rate, and only 2 percent actually purchased shirts. The following month, I sent my traditional newsletter with a small section titled "Take 10% off all Guayabera shirts! Click here to see our new line." I used only one picture of our most popular shirt and didn't include any information on price. I got a 40 percent click-through on that image alone! Less is more when it comes to e-mail marketing. Entice readers to click.

Timing and frequency

Finally, determine the appropriate consistency (daily, weekly, monthly) and delivery time (Monday morning versus Friday afternoon) for your e-mail newsletters. I am an online marketing specialist, so I check my e-mail all day long. Therefore, it's appropriate for e-mail newsletters regarding new marketing products and tips to come to me every day. However, if the other e-newsletters I subscribed to (for example, from Amazon.com or Travelocity.com) came every day, I would be overwhelmed — and be sure to unsubscribe immediately.

Instead, when I get an occasional e-mail from Amazon about a new book I might be interested in or an e-mail from

Travelocity.com about a great fare to New York City, I am much more likely to take the time to read it and react. Just like an e-mail from a distant college friend, it feels a bit more special when it only comes occasionally and when it has something specific to say.

A San Diego website, <www.SDinsider.com>, e-mails its events calendar every Wednesday night. It arrives just in time for the weekend but with enough time to forward it to all your friends who you want to invite to the local concerts and events.

At Jenny Craig, we found it most effective to send out e-mails every Monday morning. This was right after the weekend, when most dieters had strayed from their meal plans. Mondays proved an effective time to give words of encouragement and new promotions about Jenny Craig to help dieters through the week. We also gave users the option to get daily "diet tips" e-mailed to them, for those dieters who needed extra encouragement. The diet tip e-mails were one to two sentences long. Short enough for customers to read every day but long enough to keep Jenny Craig in the forefront of the customer's mind on a daily basis. (By the way, we wrote out all 365 diet tips in advance and sent them out on a timer.)

Appropriate consistency and timing differs from industry to industry. If it isn't obvious as to the best time to deliver your e-mail, just ask. When a customer subscribes to your e-mail list, ask them how often they would like to hear from you. Or send e-mail letters out different days of the week to see if there is a distinct difference in how many people actually view your newsletter on certain days.

E-Mail List Hosting Services

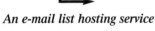

An e-mail list hosting service can make your life easier.

Thanks to e-mail hosting programs, it is easy to build, send, and track your e-mail campaigns for minimal costs. When I worked with the high-end marketing agencies, we used e-mail list hosting services such as MessageMedia's UnityMail Express. It's a great product, but also very expensive. UnityMail Express charges a one-time setup fee of $3,000, then $600 monthly.

Luckily, there are now smaller services available to help small businesses with lower budgets get their e-mail campaigns off the ground. Right now, my favorite e-mail list program is Constant

Contact. It's free for the first 50 e-mails, so it gives small businesses time to grow their list before having to commit to a monthly fee. Once the list begins to grow, the cost is still cheap, at about $10 for up to 250 names, $25 for up to 2,500 names, and so on.

Testing and templates

Using an e-mail program like Constant Contact to help you build, send, and track your e-mail newsletters is an extremely important part of marketing effectively. E-mail list hosting services not only take away the overwhelming work of manually subscribing and unsubscribing users to your database, but these services also automatically test your e-mail newsletters on all e-mail programs, such as text only, America Online (AOL), and HTML mail. They also let you choose from multiple templates, so you don't have to learn any HTML to send a colorful and professional marketing message. If you decide to use these templates, however, be sure to choose a template as close to the look and feel of your website and company brand as possible. You want all of your marketing efforts, from the color to the tone of your e-mails, to be consistent for maximum results.

Tracking success

Besides the ease of managing and sending e-mails, programs such as Constant Contact allow you to track the success of your campaign by providing reports detailing which links and images your subscribers clicked on. This allows you to know precisely which promotions and content produced the most interest and therefore which types of items to expand on in your next newsletter. The more e-mail newsletters you send out, the more refined and effective they will become. Your newsletter content should be flexible enough to evolve as you get to know your customers and track which stories, coupons, and images are motivating them to click.

Targeted content

Establish newsletter content based on your subscriber profiles. Most e-mail list services will let you set up your subscription page so that users can specify which type of content they would like to receive from you. For example, with our Baja website, we let users choose to be e-mailed "Travel alerts and road advisories," "Baja business news," "Travel coupons and specials," or "Fishing reports." By seeing how many people signed up for each list, we knew how much interest there was for each category and which areas to expand on. It also gave us more leverage to work out co-branding opportunities with related companies and in turn further expand our subscriber base.

By seeing how many people wanted travel coupons, for instance, we were able to work with a popular hotel and exchange banner ads on each other's e-mail newsletters. The hotel would offer a coupon for a free night's stay for all our website subscribers, and we'd offer "Safety Tips for Traveling in Mexico" to the hotel's mailing list. Again, we did not swap e-mail lists, but simply promoted each other's products in each other's newsletters. When you are able to truly track and identify your website's audience, it opens you up to some very cost-effective bargaining and ad swapping opportunities. (See chapter 7 for more on co-branding.)

"The secret for me," says Leni Chauvin, professional success coach and e-mail marketer, "is not to attempt to sell or push my services at all. All of my efforts go into publishing a first-class newsletter full of information that people want. This has served me well in establishing myself as an expert in my field. The newsletter is then forwarded to friends and colleagues around the world. Last count it was 68 countries! It all boils down to 'attracting versus selling.' "

That is really great advice. If your newsletter offers something of true value, like safety tips for people planning a trip to Mexico, your subscriber base will increase and your company's online brand will grow. People are much more likely to forward an interesting newsletter to their friends and family than a hard sales pitch. Establish yourself as an expert in your industry by providing your subscribers with the important information they are looking for, and they will begin to see you and your company as the only source for this type of information and service.

However, no matter how important your newsletter content may be, the content itself doesn't guarantee that your subscribers will read it. There is only one way to ensure that your e-mails don't end up in the trash: write a great subject line.

Writing an Effective Subject Line

It's a shame how many legitimate offers and great newsletters never get opened, simply because the marketer didn't take the time to write an effective subject line. After all, it's only a few words, right? How important can it be?

With more and more e-mails cluttering up all of our in-boxes daily, it's especially important to write a great subject line. In fact, your subject line is one of the most important features of your e-mail marketing efforts. It's the first impression. These few words either entice a potential customer to click on the message or cause them to hit the delete key.

Spend a disproportionate amount of time working on your subject line. After all, if your message ends up in the trash, it didn't matter how important your newsletter was.

Here is a list of rules for writing an effective subject line.

(a) *Keep it short and direct.* A subject line should never have more than ten words. Less than five words is even better. Most e-mail browsers won't let users see more than five or six words anyway, so long subject lines get lost. Don't waste space with fluffy adjectives such as "very." Use sturdy, descriptive words.

(b) *Stress the benefits to the recipient.* Make it easy for your potential customer to know exactly why they would benefit from opening your newsletter. There should be an instant "reward" or benefit for opening your message. A reward can be as simple as important information. Hinting at business results with phrases such as "save time" or "earn money" is also effective. Tease readers by telling them just enough to make them want to click and find out more.

(c) *Ask a question.* Asking a question can spark the reader's curiosity and tease them to want to know more. Also, asking a question makes the message sound more like a colleague's e-mail, so it's more likely to be opened.

(d) *Be personal.* Never send an e-mail to "Undisclosed recipients" or provide a generic auto response e-mail address as the sender. These two things scream spam. Always use a company name or a real person's name as the sender. If

Your subject line will often determine whether or not the recipient will open your e-mail. Put some thought into writing it, and test it before sending the e-mail to your customers.

you have a recognizable company name, use it; if not, use your own name. Where possible, use the recipient's name in the subject line as well as in the newsletter greeting. Most e-mail programs will automatically put the subscriber's name into the newsletter. Also, whenever possible, speak in one-to-one style. For example, "You're invited to our grand opening."

(e) *Tie in current events or holidays.* Tying in an upcoming holiday or giving your subject line a seasonal feel is very effective. Some examples: "Save money on your Christmas shopping," "Go back to school in style with these tips," or "Tips for losing 10 pounds before spring break."

(f) *Don't use the word "free."* The same rule applies to "Limited offer," "Buy now," and other hard sales terms. The reason is that many companies and Internet service providers will filter out any e-mails with such words in the subject line to avoid bogging down their systems with spam. For example, a subject line with the word "guaranteed" will be blocked by the Road Runner network. Also, be careful not to use too much hype, such as multiple exclamation marks or all caps. These make your message resemble spam and can trigger ISP filters as well.

Taking a tip from viruses

Which of these subject lines appeals to you?

- Hi! Check this.

- I love you

- Remember me?

These are all very effective subject lines because all three follow the rules described above. In fact, the only problem with these subject lines is the sender. They were all sent by viruses! Unfortunately, it seems that the people who are most successful at writing subject lines are the people sending viruses.

Most of us have fallen victim to an e-mail virus. According to an article by Ian Hopper on CNN.com, the "Love Letter" or "I LOVE YOU" bug is regarded as the biggest-ever virus case, with an estimated 15 million infected computers.

The Melissa Virus was another e-mail virus that fooled even the savviest computer users. Take a look at the subject line used:

Subject: Important Message from (username)

Here is the important document you asked for . . . don't show anyone else :-)

These virus subject lines are effective because they are personalized and entice users to want to know more. We are all curious, and if the subject line appeals to our egos ("I love you," for example), we are even more likely to want to know what the rest of the message has to say.

E-mail viruses are a terrible crime, and their proliferation has made life more difficult for legitimate e-mail marketers. People are more skeptical than ever of what is in their in-box, which is why it's more important than ever to write effective subject lines. We can learn from what works for viruses and apply their strategies to our own subject lines.

Learning what works

Below are examples of legitimate e-mails found in my in-box. Some were very effective, while others did not follow the rules described above. Can you guess which ones were successful?

From: Amazon.com

Subject: Tax Relief and a $10 Special Offer

This is an example of an effective subject line. This subject line works because, for starters, it is from "Amazon.com," which is a credible source. I have subscribed to their e-mail list, and so I am more likely to actually open the message. The subject line encourages me to click and actually read the newsletter because it's brief, it's straightforward, and it offers me a specific benefit: a $10 offer (discount/coupon) and information about tax relief (important content). Finally, the subject line is seasonal, referring to the upcoming tax season.

From: HP

Subject: *Trust* HP *to help you get your website up & running — here's a special offer!*

There are two main problems with this subject line. First, this e-mail was sent by Hewlett Packard, a very credible source. However, by abbreviating their name to HP, they lost all their credibility. With all of the viruses and junk mail out there, if it isn't completely obvious who the e-mail is from, it won't get opened. If you have a well-known, credible brand name, like Hewlett Packard, use it to your advantage; don't abbreviate. Establishing credibility and familiarity is essential in successful e-mail communications.

The second problem with this e-mail subject line is that it's far too long. Most e-mail programs will let the user see only the first five to six words. Plus, using HP in the subject line is redundant. The user already sees that the e-mail is from HP.

From: *Adobe Systems Incorporated*

Subject: *Don't Miss Out: Getting Down to Business*

This e-mail message from Adobe Systems is vague and doesn't make much sense. Remember, you have about three seconds to catch an e-mail user's attention before your promotion ends up in the trash. Be straightforward and tell them exactly what to expect. Adobe Systems actually did have a really great offer in this e-mail (a free half-day offline seminar aimed at small businesses), but because of the vague subject line, most people missed it. Heidi Anderson, in her April 2002 *ClickZ* article titled "E-mail Testing: Here Come the Bridesmaids," examined the importance of subject lines. In her article, she presents the example of Dessy

Creations, a major retailer of bridesmaid dresses in Manhattan (see Case Study).

As Dessy Creations did, testing your subject lines and e-mail newsletters definitely pays off. It takes a little extra time, but the results are worth it. Whether it's a small group of your friends or just a small percentage of your e-mail list, sending out a test message will not only eliminate some of those first-time jitters, but really let you zone in on what types of promotions are working for your business. Doing this type of online testing beforehand is especially important if you plan to spend money on expensive offline promotions such as magazine or newspaper ads. Internet testing is very cheap and usually takes only your time, not your dollars.

Creating a successful e-newsletter comes with practice. Each industry expects different things from a newsletter, just as different formulas work better for different types of businesses. Some of us have customers that are more computer literate than others; some have fast Internet connections while others are still on dial-up. Some check e-mail every day at work, while others only check once a week from home. Knowing your audience is essential to creating and sending effective e-mail marketing messages.

I am pretty confident that you have a flood of personal e-mails, business questions, jokes, spam, junk mail, and maybe even a couple of viruses in your e-mail in-box right now. Take a moment to examine which e-mails entice you to read on and which ones you automatically delete. Of the marketing e-mails you do open, which ones encourage you to click through to that company's website? Which e-mail newsletters did you actually subscribe to and why? Getting ideas from your own in-box is a great way to start building ideas for your own business e-mail communications.

Here are the results of two different Dessy Creations e-mail campaigns, outlined by Heidi Anderson in *ClickZ:*

Campaign Number One

Dessy Creations, a major retailer of bridesmaid dresses, wanted to promote its new online ordering feature, especially targeted at residents of Manhattan, where their storefront was located. To test the impact of two different subject lines, they divided their e-mail list

CASE STUDY

into two groups. Below are the two subject lines. Can you guess which subject line generated the most results?

> **Subject Line 1:** *Live in Manhattan? Buy your bridesmaid dress online!*
>
> **Subject Line 2:** *Manhattan Residents: Buy your bridesmaid dress online!*

Subject line 1 far outperformed the second one, with a whopping four times as many click-throughs to the website. The reason? For one thing, the first subject line asks a question, which gets the customer involved and sparks curiosity. Also, the question gives subject line 1 a friendlier and more inviting tone, while subject line 2 sounds more like a command. Remember, it's all about "attracting versus selling" or, in other words, "enticing versus telling." Which explains why subject line 1 was more effective than subject line 2.

Campaign Number Two

This time, Dessy decided to test the content of the newsletter rather than the subject line. Dessy offered the same promotion in each newsletter, the key difference being the image used. In the first mailing, the graphic was small, with the idea that people don't like to wait for heavy downloads. In the second mailing, a much larger graphic was used. Guess what? The larger graphic was more than twice as effective.

Dessy followed up by sending the e-mail with the larger graphic to the entire e-mail list and was more than pleased with the results. Before the mailing, sales averaged about two to four dresses per day. After the e-mail, sales jumped to 10 to 20 dresses per day. When it comes to a product like clothing or jewelry, larger graphics are more effective. People want to see as much detail as possible before making this type of purchase.

Use Worksheet 2 to brainstorm ideas for monthly e-mail promotions for your company.

Worksheet 2
PLANNING YOUR E-MAIL CAMPAIGN

Chapter 5 examined the importance of relevancy and timing in your e-mail promotions and newsletters. Ideally, you should be sending out some type of e-mail communication once a month, promoting a new special or bit of information to keep customers interested in hearing from you and coming back to your website. It's always a good idea to plan out your e-mail campaigns ahead of time, so you can budget and plan for any season promotions you may want to do. Also, remember to update your home page with the same promotion you are e-mailing out to your customers.

Below, brainstorm a seasonal promotion you could e-mail out for each month. In order to help you make it relevant to the season, I've included popular holidays and themes for each month.

January: _____
(New Year's resolutions, health & weight loss, budgeting after the holidays, Martin Luther King, Jr. holiday)

February: _____
(Valentine's Day, President's weekend)

March: _____
(St. Patrick's Day, Spring Break for many colleges)

April: _____
(Spring, Easter, April Fool's Day)

May: _____
(Mother's Day, Cinco de Mayo, Memorial Day)

June: _____
(Summer, school holidays, Father's Day)

July: _____
(4th of July, picnics, summer vacations)

August: _____
(Summer heat, children home from school)

Worksheet 2 — Continued

September: _____
(Back to school, Fall)

October: _____
(Halloween, Columbus Day)

November: _____
(Thanksgiving, fall harvest, elections)

December: _____
(Christmas, Hanukkah, Winter, New Year's Eve, holiday parties)

CHAPTER 6
BUILDING AN ONLINE COMMUNITY

Ninety-two percent of the web population frequents some type of online community. That's 95 million users, or 1 out of every 3 Americans (Nielsen//NetRatings, June 2001). What makes online communities so attractive to so many people? For starters, they are the virtual equivalent of a local bar, coffee shop, or any other place where people with similar interests can meet someone new or learn something new. Online communities are places where people can anonymously find others with the same fears, problems, and interests. They are places where people can confirm their beliefs or find more fuel for their arguments by chatting with other like-minded people. They are places where those facing hardship or loss can find solace or advice from others going through the same thing.

What Are Online Communities and Why Are They Important?

Online communities should ultimately be a place of familiarity and comfort that can be accessed from anywhere at any time. They most often consist of message boards, chatrooms, event calendars, newsletters, and anything else that lets users with common interests interact on a personal or anonymous level.

Building your own online community can provide you with a highly targeted audience.

Why is providing a sense of community important for your small business? Customers who participate in online communities represent a highly attractive sales target because of their high affinity for product loyalty on their favorite community sites. Research provided by Lithium Technologies states that "Members of online customer communities have an average sales volume representing 500% of that of the average company customers."

Community-based websites such as <www.eBay.com>, <www.iVillage.com>, and <www.women.com> are proving so successful that according to the Gartner Group (July 2001), "By 2005, more than 50 percent of enterprises will include community features as part of their customer service strategy."

When you build a strong customer community, you've built loyalty in your company, products, and services. Loyal customers generate new customers through word of mouth, which increases sales further. Encouraging your existing customers to e-mail coupons or sign up their friends and family for your newsletter further increases your customer base.

Community-Building Technology and Ideas

Amazon.com has been encouraging community building since the site first launched in July 1995. One of the final steps when making a purchase on Amazon.com is the opportunity to send a coupon for that same product to a friend. The most popular book site has not missed a beat in the community-building process. Loyal customers even help sell Amazon's products to complete strangers in the website's "Spotlight Reviews" section. In the review section, customers provide genuine testimonials and feedback on products, helping new customers finalize their purchasing decision.

Message boards

Small businesses can encourage similar community building by providing a moderated forum such as a message board. By dividing your message board into product categories and encouraging customers to share their opinions, you've taken the first step in building a community. Message boards not only help increase sales through real customer recommendations, but can also significantly cut down on customer service costs, since many customers will answer each other's questions. Just be sure to moderate your message board regularly to ensure your customers are getting the right information. I suggest checking it daily, or more often it is an extremely busy message board.

Providing a forum for customers to discuss your products and services also allows you to gain honest feedback about your products and company, which in turn will allow you to better respond to real customers' needs. In addition, knowing more about who your customer is can markedly reduce customer acquisition costs, because you will have a clearer idea of who your best customers are.

An active message board is an essential part of a successful online community. The first thing I look at before I post a message to a message board is the date of the last post. If I take the time to post something here, will anyone respond? A highly active message board is the reason that a simple Baja California traveler's website called Bajanet was BajaPortal.com's biggest competitor. Bajanet was not a pretty site, and it wasn't even updated that often. But it was the most talked about and visited site among Baja enthusiasts due to the high traffic and quality posts on its message boards. No matter how many new Baja-related websites emerged, Bajanet continued to have the most loyal following of Baja travelers, simply because of the success of its community-based message boards.

Basic message boards can be implemented very cheaply, sometimes even for free. Start by asking your current website hosting company if they have a message board feature that you can add to your existing hosting package. If not, try a simple search on the Internet for "free message boards." Most likely, you'll be able to find active examples of the message boards. Go ahead and click around the message boards. Most likely, you'll find real customer reviews of the board and advice on whether or not it's right for your business.

Content

Successful online communities are much more than a message board. The type of content your website provides often determines the quality of your online community. The professionalism of your website content directs the topics on the message boards and sets the tone of your website as a whole. Content is the first thing that attracts your audience and the primary factor shaping their decision to become a part of your community. Forums, message boards, and chatrooms are all ways users can respond to your content.

Website content is key to the success of an online community.

When you have an active online community, new content ideas begin flowing. You'll know exactly what type of information your customers are looking for and how to respond. A message board can be a way of generating custom content that changes daily. Having an active message board of customer questions and suggestions is a low-maintenance, low-cost way for people to see new things each time they visit your site. As I've said, just be sure to consistently monitor your message board so that the conversations continue in the positive direction you've intended.

Calendars

Calendars are also an important part of online communities because they help fuel community spirit and give users a chance to meet offline. Even if your company does not have any events going on offline, providing a calendar of events that would interest your audience positions you as an industry leader and a reliable source for industry information. For example, if you are a real estate agent, perhaps you could post dates of an upcoming seminar about how to get a home loan. Or perhaps there is a local workshop on do-it-yourself kitchens. Event listings are a helpful, informative form of community building content that will encourage repeat visits to your site.

Contests

Another fun way to get users excited about your website is to have a contest. Contests should encourage users to share a story about your product or how your service helped them in some way. After the contest is over, post the stories and winners' names on the website. This material serves as a customer testimonial as well as a great way to get insight into your customers' lives.

I recently added a similar contest to a small, family-owned winery's website, <www.zuccawines.com>. Zucca Mountain Vineyards does a great job of having their customers help them create content through their recipe contest. On their home page, they have a banner that says, "Submit a recipe and win two free bottles of Zucca Wine." They post the winning recipes under their food pairing section along with the customer's name. This shows a sense of community as well as loyalty to their customers, and the contest gives every visitor a chance to be a part of the site. Putting together a simple contest like this does not require any special technology — just access to your e-mail and someone who can post the winning results on the website.

Chatrooms

One popular community feature that I do not recommend for small businesses is a chatroom. Chatrooms are tough to get going. Unless you have a very large audience, like more than 100,000 regular users per month, a chatroom just won't work. If you do have a large number of active users, always schedule a chat rather than leaving your chatroom open. This is easier to monitor and keeps the conversations targeted and interesting. I've found the best success with DigiChat or ParaChat, online software programs you pay a monthly fee to use on your website.

LivePerson instant messaging

Speedy communication with your web audience can mean the difference between closing and losing a sale. If you or your employees spend a majority of your business day in front of the computer, I recommend looking into a program such as LivePerson <www.liveperson.com> which is similar to AOL's Instant Messenger. These programs let you instantly communicate with your customers. Picture this: you are shopping on your favorite gift website for that perfect bottle of wine for a special occasion, but you don't know much about wine. Short on time, you click on the "Click here for live help!" button. A customer service representative on the other end gets an alert message on her computer screen.

"How can I help you today" the customer service rep types back.

"I want to find the perfect red wine for a dinner party. The host will be serving filet mignon."

"Sure, I can help you. What is your price range?"

"I can spend up to $50 per bottle."

"Here are the links to three of our most popular red wines that go well with red meat. Plus, here is the link to a $10 off gift certificate for your second bottle."

In a matter of seconds, the customer service rep closes the sale, and the customer feels as if he or she has made an educated choice as well as gotten a great deal, at $10 off.

With LivePerson, your employees can chat instantly with multiple customers at once and save costs on phone calls at the same time. LivePerson now offers an affordable small-business version of their regular technology, called LivePerson Pro. Check their website for current prices and details.

Community Editors

Maintaining an online community can be a lot of work. While running our Baja website, there was no way our small staff could have kept up with all the different sections of our large web community. So we used volunteer editors for each section. For example, we'd have someone who was in charge of all fishing content and related message board posts. That way, we'd have an expert in each field who was truly excited about the topic. Often, we would let the guest editors plug their own products in exchange for monitoring a section of the message board.

iVillage, the top women's community portal, uses a similar approach. iVillage encourages regular users to sign up as "community leaders" in the section of their choice. Hopefuls submit an application and sign a basic contract agreeing to participate in a one-hour chatroom training program and spend at least one hour a week answering message board posts. From the moment you log on to <www.iVillage.com>, you have the option of finding other women just like you. From the home page, you can jump directly to mini sites complete with interesting articles, message boards, and so on for women "In Your 30s," "In Your 20s," "Stay-at-Home Moms," and dozens of other women-focused community groups.

Get your entire staff involved in your online community and recognize them publicly by name often. This will put a name and maybe even a face (if you include personal bios with photos) to your community. The key to a successful online community is investing in the time to plan it out according to your goals and to train your staff on how to respond to particular posts or responses. In the beginning, you and your staff will need to answer every post and even plant some of your own questions and comments to get the message board flowing. As your traffic builds, the message board and other community features will begin to take on a life of their own, and your staff can simply oversee them.

Buying Ad Space on Other Community Websites

If you don't have the time or resources to keep up with managing a community website, then the next best thing is to purchase ad space on an already established, high-profile community that makes sense for your product. According to an October 2002 study by Online Publishers Association (OPA), the feeling a regular user has for their favorite community site influences their perceptions of that site's advertisers. Of the 4,982 survey participants, most said that they were less annoyed by advertising on sites they liked, and reported these sites as less ad cluttered. Also, audiences with a high affinity to a community website reported stronger brand loyalty and a willingness to pay more for products they perceived to be of higher quality.

Purchasing ad space on another online community's site may be an effective alternative to building your own community.

A related analysis conducted by Media Metrix reported that the top 40 percent of a website's users account for 85 percent of all page impressions (aka exposures). This means that the more someone uses a website, the more familiar he or she becomes with its advertisers, and therefore associates the two. Another analysis, by Dynamic Logic, found that more ad exposures — up to five — resulted in increased message association. If frequency of exposure equals advertising effectiveness, this would seem to mean that loyal users are most likely to respond to your advertising message.

But not all community sites produce equal results. The OPA study found that sites with original content had a higher percentage of visitors who responded positively to ads within the network than their portal counterparts with no original content. For example, a financial site such as <www.MarketWatch.com> with original content has more higher-affinity viewers than, say, Yahoo! Finance. So choose your community ad buys accordingly.

CHAPTER 7

CO-BRANDING STRATEGIES

Picture this: it's late Wednesday afternoon and you've been in back-to-back client meetings all day. You head to the nearest Starbucks for a quick pick-me-up before you go back to the office. While you're waiting for your favorite coffee drink, you hear the smooth sounds of a brand new jazz artist playing over the café speakers. You immediately look down to notice the cardboard counter display box with a "Now Playing" sign over a stack of CDs published by Hear Music.

When Hear Music teamed up with Starbucks in 1999, they formed a co-branded partnership. The partnership works because the brands enhance each other's product rather than compete. The musical compilations, "dedicated to helping people discover all the great music beyond the Top 40," enhance the shopping experience at Starbucks while giving the coffee chain a more sophisticated appeal.

Why Co-Branding Is Different Online

In the real world, the layout of retail co-branding can be pretty straightforward. In the previous example, staff simply set up a display box of Hear Music compilation CDs on every Starbucks coffee counter. However, implementing co-branding activities effectively on the web is much more complicated.

In a Starbucks outlet, no one fears touching a Hear Music CD and instantly finding themselves standing in the Hear Music warehouse in Cambridge, Massachusetts. But on the web, this fear is a (virtual) reality. If someone clicks on a link and is taken to a web page with a different feeling or brand, the result can be disorienting — and disastrous if you lose a customer as a result. A user should never wonder "What happened? "Where am I?" when clicking on something on your website. For this reason, how you choose to display your partnerships online is just as important as the type of partnership you develop.

Co-branding is great for the pocketbook and can be especially beneficial for small businesses. But choosing the wrong partners or too many partners can cause more harm than good. This chapter explores the right and wrong ways of co-branding online and why joint ventures and promotions are especially important for your small-business online marketing plan.

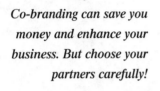

Co-branding can save you money and enhance your business. But choose your partners carefully!

Integrating Partnerships into Your Website

The following example shows that even some of the "big guys" online don't always successfully integrate their partners. When the popular search engine Lycos teamed up with several online retailers, such as RedEnvelope.com and CatalogCity.com, the result was user frustration and confusion. Rather than taking the necessary steps to truly integrate RedEnvelope's gift content into the Lycos Shopping site, Lycos simply slapped their navigation on a RedEnvelope page, leaving users to wonder if they had left the Lycos site altogether.

On the other hand, if a user clicks on Lycos's "clothing" tab, they are transported to the <www.CatologCity.com> website with a Lycos header. All of the original shopping navigation that was once on Lycos now belongs to CatologCity.com. Lycos would be better off simply linking to these websites than trying to frame the partner's site within its own. Once the user gets confused, both partners have lost out.

In contrast, when Amazon.com added Target's products to its online store, they provided clear Target-style branding combined with the comfort of Amazon's familiar shopping cart. Log on to <www.Amazon.com> and you'll see one of the main navigation buttons with the familiar red and white Target logo. Click through and you are clearly still on Amazon's site, but have access to all of Target's products.

When AskJeeves.com integrated 20th Century Fox and Dreamworks' new movie *Cast Away* into the look and feel of the site, the result was a pleasant surprise. AskJeeves.com transformed its entire home page into a *Cast Away* theme, complete with the famous Wilson volleyball bouncing across the home page. The familiar AskJeeves.com character traded in his stuffy suit for vacation-style clothing, all in alignment with the movie theme. The movie *Cast Away* and the popular search engine in no way competed with each other, and the design did an effective job of integrating the two products. While Lycos and its shopping partners appear to fight for branding dominance, AskJeeves.com and its movie partner seamlessly integrated to create excitement about both brands.

Although AskJeeves.com and *Cast Away* made for a very cool online promotion, small businesses need to be more careful with their marketing dollars. Although doing something cool and innovative usually gets media attention, small businesses need to make sure they will see a direct result from the partnership, whether it is increased web traffic, online sales, or customer contact information. Remember, general branding is expensive online. Stick to trackable results, and find partners who can help you get them.

With that said, co-branding, also referred to as joint ventures, joint promotions, value endorsements, and alliances, works best when both companies provide distinctly different services or products but share similar audiences. An example is the very successful marketing partnership between Sony PlayStation and Red Bull energy drink; both companies appeal to teenage boys yet offer very different products.

The Power of Co-Branding

The bottom line is that consumers actually like co-branding. It helps them to decide among the hundreds of brands out there. The American Marketing Association released a study further emphasizing this concept (cited by Martin Lindstrom in *ClickZ*). The study found that when appropriate, two brands pushing a product are much better than one. In the study, 80 percent of those surveyed said they would buy a digital imaging product if it were co-branded by Sony and Kodak. However, only 20 percent said they would buy the same digital imaging product if it was made by only Sony or only Kodak.

According to Lindstrom, in another study, published by the *Journal of Consumer Marketing* in 2000, the power of co-branding was confirmed in a taste test of potato chips and dips. In the first taste test trial, researchers attached a well-known brand name to both the bag of chips and the carton of dip. In the second trial, they served the test group the exact same chips and dip, but used a fictional brand name. The researchers also tested the response to name-brand chips combined with a fictional-brand dip and vice versa. The result? The participants rated the name-brand chips and dip combination significantly higher than any other combination of high and low brands.

For co-branding to work, the consumer must be able to perceive the relationship between the two brands

This study concluded that when high-quality brands team up together, the co-branding strengthens consumers' approval rating. Furthermore, if an unknown brand teams up with an already established popular brand, the partnership, if done right, will not only help increase the unknown brand's sales, but also strengthen that brand. The study also found that if a popular brand teams up with an unknown brand, it will not hurt the popular brand (as long as they keep a close eye on the quality of the customer service and product of the lower brand), but sales won't necessarily be increased either. The best bet for a strong brand is to team up with an equal partner.

However, like chips and dip, co-branding partnerships must make sense. If it isn't completely obvious why two companies should partner up, the benefit to the consumer won't be obvious either. For example, the 1998 AT&T and British Telecom alliance, which was backed by more than $10 billion, failed in less than two years. It seems consumers couldn't quite grasp the connection between the two mega brands.

Co-Branding Guidelines

The failure of AT&T's co-branding partnership with British Telecom shows that successful co-branding is not about how large your budget is, but rather how appropriate the synergy is between the two brands. Co-branding provides a perfect avenue for small businesses. With the right partner, you can share marketing costs, technologies, and resources; strengthen your brand; and gain access to a whole new customer base, all with one well-thought-out campaign. But before contacting a potential partner or planning your next campaign, give some serious thought to the following co-branding guidelines:

(a) What will the brand partnership say about the customer? Will the partnership make the customer feel more educated? More classy? More hip?

(b) What characteristics do the two brands and the consumer share? Are they both innovative? Cutting-edge? Dependable? Make sure that your new campaign image does not clash with the image your current customer base has of your company. You never want to lose that current base, just build on it.

(c) What benefit does the brand partnership provide to the customer? Does it save them time or money? Make the immediate benefit to the customer very clear in your campaign.

(d) Is the partnership user centered? Is your goal to provide the best solution to the customer? It should be.

(e) Is there an equal value for both brands involved? The relationship must be equal or it just won't work.

(f) Is the value of the partnership easy for customers to understand?

(g) Does the partnership open up your company to new customers? Will it help you upsell your current customers?

If you don't seriously think about all these questions, your partnership could do your company more harm than good. Co-branding and joint promotions take time and energy to implement, but when done correctly, they deliver results that can far outweigh more traditional online advertising, such as banner ads.

An eMarketer study cited by Lindstrom in *ClickZ* found that the percentage of online marketing ad dollars spent on banner ads shrank from 52 percent in 1998 to 26 percent in 2001. At the same time, sponsorship-type ad campaigns were estimated to have increased from 40 percent to 58 percent. In other words, more and more companies are finding positive results in sponsorship/co-branding campaigns.

Co-branding, if done well, can be more effective than traditional forms of advertising.

According to Bobbie Halfin in her March 1999 *ClickZ* article, the basic rule of online advertising success is to "bring your content, promotion, and/or message to where the customer is, instead of focusing 100 percent of your energy on the difficult (and often unsuccessful) task of diverting consumers to your site and away from the place they've chosen to be."

With this concept in mind, Toyota launched an integrated marketing campaign to promote its 2003 4Runner (see Case Study). Obviously the 4Runner campaign is an example of co-branding at a much larger scale than most companies could ever hope to compete with. Small businesses can't be expected to generate product buzz by trekking to the top of Mount Everest. However, this example shows how much reach and power can be gained by choosing the appropriate partners to help you push that buzz, no matter how large or small it may be. Toyota strategically chose partners such as popular weather sites, Mobliss wireless, and a top portal like Yahoo! to ensure that their buzz was passed around the specific target audience they intended.

CASE STUDY

For its integrated marketing campaign to promote its 2003 4Runner, the Toyota marketing team organized a video and photo shoot at the 17,262-foot-elevation base camp of Mount Everest. Michael Bush reported on DMNews.com that images from the four-day journey to the base camp of Mount Everest became a primary part of the car company's online ad campaign. In order to reach "the new generation of outdoor adventurers," Toyota teamed up with top news, sports, and weather websites to ensure that no one in their target market (technology-savvy, computer-literate outdoor adventurers) would miss the rugged new images of the 2003 4Runner. Toyota also signed exclusive sponsorship deals dominating the weather category and snow reports for Mobliss wireless alerts in addition to dominating placement deals with top weather websites such as <www.weather.com>, <www.accuweather.com>, and <www.weatherbug.com>.

Toyota.com carries the outdoor, rugged adventure theme throughout its website by posting a new adventure story each month. The website's destination section features 50 off-road adventures, offering readers tips and advice for planning their own adventure. Toyota took the campaign even further by teaming up with Yahoo! to promote its television show *Global Extremes: Mount Everest — 4Runner Adventures.* The Global Extremes website <www.yahoo.com/globalextremes> included athlete profiles, competition updates, and video highlights, allowing users to track each step of the athletes' journeys through the competition on the website and wireless phones.

Rather than simply buying banner ads or television commercial spots, Toyota has taken the idea of product placement and completely immersed it in the virtual world. Toyota's effective use of content generation, co-branding partnerships, and ability to generate a product buzz among its target audience makes for an extremely well-rounded online campaign. And the fact that they have integrated their print, outdoor, and television ads with their Internet campaign strengthens the 4Runner's brand as a dominant car of choice for the younger, tech-savvy generation.

Here's an example of a co-branded campaign at a smaller scale. Alloy Online simply used the power of "free stuff" to generate a buzz about their company. Alloy Online, whose target audience is 10- to 24-year-old girls, joined forces with *Seventeen* magazine's website to create a powerful online brand targeting teen girls. By sponsoring sweepstakes and contests on *Seventeen* magazine's website, the company quickly established itself as a key player in the teen market. Alloy was able to show positive return on investment by focusing each of its "free stuff" campaigns on the following goals:

  ▶ Strengthening Alloy's brand identity with teen girls through its association with *Seventeen* magazine

- Building its e-mail list through online contest registrations
- Creating an overall excitement through creative product giveaways, which in turn encourage "word of mouth" and viral marketing activities
- Increasing overall traffic to the Alloy.com website

"As a leading Internet site for teens, we are very selective in how and where we spend our online ad dollars," Alloy's vice president of Business Development, Andrew Roberts, told Bobbie Halfin in her 1999 interview for *ClickZ*. "With banners alone, it's very difficult to create a strong emotional connection to our brand without completely partnering with a site. When advertising on other sites, we realize that our targeted user has self-selected that destination. Our goal is to find the best way to involve them with the Alloy brand on another site's turf."

How to Integrate Partner Products

Alloy did an effective job of really integrating their product into the *Seventeen* magazine website <www.seventeen.com>, which made users more receptive to the promotions. It's important to take the time to incorporate the benefits of both brands into the design as well as the text of the promotion, so that your audience clearly understands the connection.

Do it right the first time

When Sephora launched its 1999 website with co-branding in mind, the result was a website that was confusing and inconsistent. As detailed on Internet World, the 1999 Sephora website included different levels of co-branding for each of its product lines. Click on the "Make up" or "Bath and Body" link and you were taken to a page with appropriate products and logos. But click on the logos, and sometimes you were taken to a page with more of that specific company's products, while other times you were taken to an animated flash commercial. Users were continually thrown into different user interfaces depending on which company logo they clicked on. As in the Lycos Shopping example, simply putting another company's logo or products within your website without truly taking the time to integrate it will severely hamper the overall user experience.

Slapping your logo or navigation on someone else's content may save money and time in the short term, but it will cost you potential customers in the long run. Good co-branding should never make the user wonder whose website they are on. It should enhance a shopping experience, by helping that shopper make a more informed decision. The new Sephora.com website does a much more effective job of combining all of their partners' logos and branding into one consistent and easy to understand website. Exchanging content with your co-branding partner is a great way for both companies to expand credibility in your industry. However, as demonstrated by the Sephora and Lycos examples, you must take the extra time to incorporate the content into the look and feel of your website. The result will be more powerful, because the content will look less like an advertisement and more like essential, professional content that your customers can benefit from.

Take a tip from newspapers

Think of your local newspaper or even your favorite news website. Only a small percentage of the news stories are actually generated by in-house staff. Most likely the rest come from the AP Newswire. The newspaper then formats those stories to look like the rest of its pages. Can you imagine if every story written by an independent news source or freelance writer was formatted differently? You would have a hard time differentiating the advertisements from the new stories from the editorials and so on. On the Internet, such design inconsistencies are detrimental to a user's experience. In the virtual world, unlike the real world, it's easy to get confused as to where you are and who is giving you the information.

Complementary Partnerships Work Best

Well-integrated co-branded content will make your site appear more well-rounded, legitimate, complete, and competitive. Just remember that co-branded content will only help your business if it complements your general business goals. Don't lose sight of what you are trying to accomplish online, whether it's online sales, credibility, or new clients. Make sure that all your content, promotions, and partnership activities encourage visitors to take the actions you've intended.

So what are you waiting for? Grab your business partners and employees and start brainstorming which companies you'd like to team up with. Then narrow that list down to the ones that really make sense. Remember, smart marketers look for a few strong partners to build ongoing relationships with. Too many partners can muddy your brand and confuse your existing customers. Once you've confirmed your list of ideal partners, package your ideas in a way that shows benefit to that potential partner. Make it easy for a company to team up with you on projects. Be flexible and listen to what the other company's goals are: for a joint promotion to work, both companies have to find equal benefit in the partnership.

Use Worksheet 3 to plan a proposal you can send to companies you'd like to have as co-branding partners.

Worksheet 3
FINDING THE RIGHT CO-BRANDING PARTNER

1. Brainstorm at least ten products or services that would complement your product or service. (Think about products or services that people usually purchase together; for example, a carpenter could team up with a painter, or a web designer could team up with a hosting company.)

   1. _____
   2. _____
   3. _____
   4. _____
   5. _____
   6. _____
   7. _____
   8. _____
   9. _____
   10. _____

2. Circle the top two products or services that could enhance your company's brand, reach, and credibility. Now think of some companies that offer those products and services with which you could realistically team up.

   1. _____
   2. _____
   3. _____
   4. _____
   5. _____

3. Brainstorm some promotions you could do with these products.

   _____
   _____
   _____
   _____

4. What would be the estimated costs of a co-branded campaign such as this?

   _____

   _____

   _____

   _____

5. What types of services could you offer in exchange for monetary contributions?

   _____

   _____

   _____

   _____

6. How would success of the campaign be measured? In overall sales? In new customers? In media attention?

   _____

   _____

   _____

   _____

   _____

   Create a well-thought-out, professional proposal based on the information you have brainstormed above, and send it to the top company with which you would like to partner on a marketing campaign. If your top choice rejects your offer, contact your second choice, and so on. Good luck!

CHAPTER 8

GETTING TO THE TOP OF THE SEARCH ENGINES

In previous chapters I've talked about word of mouth, viral marketing, and e-mail marketing, but the most common way people find new websites, products, and services is through search engines.

According to Greg Jarboe in his April 2004 article for Clickz.com, "Journalists now use the Internet as easily as the phone. For article research, 92% of journalists working at newspaper, magazine, and broadcast outlets nationwide go online — and 81% say they search online daily."

This means that whether you are looking to sell your products online or even just generate some press about your service, your website must be found by the search engines. And not just any search engines — the top search engines. At the time this book was published, Google and Yahoo! had the strongest hold on the search engine market capturing more than 25 percent of the marketing share, followed by MSN and AOL with 10 percent. Excite, Ask Jeeves, and InfoSpace hold a little more than 1 percent while other search engines such as AltaVista, AllTheWeb, HotBot, Lycos, Netscape, and Teoma hold less than 1 percent.

Please note that top search engines partner up on occasion, use similar technologies, or even outsource specific searches to each other if their own technology doesn't have adequate results. Many are part of an ad network such as Overture, which allows the top three positions to be taken by the highest bidder (there is more on this later in the chapter). And just when you think you've got it all figured out, everything seems to change! Google will strike a new deal with Yahoo! or Overture will add new partners to its network. It is a full-time job simply keeping up with all the nuances and changes in search technology. However, don't despair. When your website is designed correctly, a search engine can be a small business's best weapon in acquiring more traffic. Just be sure to follow this chapter's basic rules of website optimization to ensure that you're not sabotaging your efforts before you even begin.

How to Optimize Your Website

The most important thing to consider when optimizing your website for search engine success is that search engines read text, not graphics. Websites with Flash intros or graphic-heavy home pages are at a disadvantage from the start. When it comes to top search engine rankings, simple sites that place an emphasis on text rank best.

Choosing the right keywords

Keyword phrases are what Internet users type into a search engine to find relevant products and services. They are typically two to three words long.

Before spending the time to optimize your site, it's a good idea to use a program like WordTracker.com, Microsoft Small Business Center, or Overture.com to help you determine which keyword phrases have the highest search volume. That way you can make sure your efforts are spent optimizing for the *right* keywords.

Microsoft Small Business Center charges a small fee to use its search engine submission service. Before you submit your site, it lets you enter keyword phrases and determine which options have the highest search volume.

Overture advertisers have access to recommended keyword phrases and search volumes when they select "add listings" to their accounts or set up a new account.

Finally, WordTracker.com is a paid service that not only gives you a breakdown of your keyword phrases by search volume, but takes it a step further by telling you how much competition there is for each phrase. This way, you can find the keyword phrase with the highest search volume and least amount of competition.

Home page text

Once you have determined the best keywords to use, the next step is to put those keyword phrases within the content of your website. Pay extra attention to the first paragraph on your home page, as search engines most often read the first few lines of a site to determine its relevancy to a user's search. Use as many keywords and phrases as possible in that first paragraph to ensure your site comes up when a user searches for those particular keywords. For example, here is the first paragraph on my website, <www.berkweb.com>:

You can attract more viewers to your website with savvy use of home-page text, HTML tags, and by going easy on Flash pages and graphics.

> *Berkley Web Strategies is a collection of top San Diego website designers, business consultants, and online marketing specialists working together to give your company the highest-quality website possible.*
>
> *Each team of web designers and online marketing consultants is chosen based on individual client needs so that you get exactly what you want. Services include website development, Internet Marketing and Strategy, E-commerce Solutions, Search Engine Optimization and Registration, E-mail Marketing, Custom Database Programming, Flash Animation, Content Development, Site Maintenance, website Hosting, E-mail Accounts, and much more!*

The above paragraph not only gives an introduction to my company's services, but also includes all of the keywords that a potential customer might use when searching for a web design or online marketing consultant.

HTML tags

Next, you'll need to make sure your web designer included the appropriate tags in your HTML code that correspond with your website text. Remember, the more consistent your text and tags are, the more solid your ranking will be. Following are the types of tags that are important for search engine positioning, as well as a good example of what that tag should look like in your HTML code. I have continued to use my own website tags as an example, so you can see how all of the pieces match up. For example, the important keywords such as "web designer" and "online marketing consultant" are repeated throughout.

Title tag

The title tag is the first sentence an Internet user will see when your website comes up in a search. Be sure your title tag includes both keywords and a solid marketing message that will encourage users to click to your site.

> ***Example:*** *<title> Berkley Web Strategies — website design, Online marketing, Internet consulting </title>*

Meta tags

Meta tags are keywords and phrases inserted into the code of your web page that are not viewable to the user, but are viewable to the search engines. Most search engines use a technology called "spiders" or "web crawlers" to find and index web pages. Spiders crawl across your entire web page, making sure that meta tags match the regular text on your site. The more consistent your tags are with your actual site content, the better.

At one time, meta tags were a primary factor in ranking websites. Unfortunately, many website owners and marketers began taking advantage of the system and began repeating the same keywords excessively throughout their meta tags, hoping to trick search engines into ranking them higher. The result was a less valuable search for the end user. For this reason, top search engines such as Excite and Lycos quietly dropped this category from their search engine ranking technology, while newer search engines such as Google and FAST never added the requirement at all.

Jon Glick, AltaVista's director of Internet Search, told Danny Sullivan in an October 2002 *ClickZ* article, "In the past, we have indexed meta keyword tags but have found that the high incidence of keyword repetition and spam made it an unreliable indication of site content and quality. We do continue to look at this issue and may re-include [meta tags] if the perceived quality improves over time."

Although meta tags are not as essential to ranking as they were in the early nineties, it doesn't hurt to continue to implement them. My advice on meta tags is to add them anyway. After all, there are still smaller search engines that could pick you up.

> *Example:* *<meta name="keywords" content="Berkley Web Strategies, website development, Internet consultant, online marketing, website design, web design, web designer, San Diego web designer, California web designer, web page design">*

ALT tags

Have you ever rolled your mouse over an image on a website and seen a box of text pop up? That text is called an ALT tag. ALT tags identify by text what the image is. Since search engines don't read graphics, by adding ALT tags, you are adding a text element that search engines can read. ALT tags allow all computers to know exactly what is on your site, no matter what type of platform they are using.

Technology such as Bobby <bobby.watchfire.com/> was designed with ALT tags in mind so that people with disabilities can use the Internet. For example, a visually impaired person using the Internet would have a special browser that reads the ALT tags to let him or her know what is on that page. It is especially important to include ALT tags on your main navigation so disabled users can know where to click to get their information.

Keep image tags brief. They should be no more than a short phrase, long enough to include your keywords, but effective enough to actually describe your image to disabled users. To find out if your website is viewable to disabled users, visit the Bobby website <bobby.watchfire.com/> and type in your URL. The site gives you a quick printout of problems your site may have.

> *Example:* *<img src="office_building.gif" alt="Our San Diego Web Design Office">*

Flash pages, image maps, and heavy graphics

Websites that use a lot of heavy graphics or Flash animation have a hard time being recognized by the search engines. Ideally, search engines like to see at least 200 words of related text (text that matches your title tags, meta-tags, and so on). Placement of your text is also key. Heavy graphics, animation, and JavaScript can push important text way down in the coding of your web page.

To check how far down your home page text starts, simply view your source code (right-click with your mouse and select "view source"). Are lengthy lines of JavaScript and other complex code pushing your important, keyword-loaded text toward the bottom of the page? If so, this could be hurting your rankings. To avoid this, opt for plain HTML text links rather than graphics- and code-heavy image maps. Keep overall web page graphics light and keep important text toward the top of the page.

Flash pages simply cannot be read by search engines. However, Flash pages can be a very effective part of your website. Your best bet is to embed a small flash movie within your regular HTML page. Or better yet, provide a simple HTML link to your Flash movie. Never design your home page entirely in Flash.

It's frustrating, for web designers especially, to learn that their innovative work and imagination won't be the first thing that captures a user's attention when they visit a site. But it's the simpler sites that get the highest ranking on the search engines. For small businesses with limited budgets, it's even more important to abide by the search engine rules if you ever hope to compete for the same traffic as the big guys.

For some businesses, however, it just doesn't make sense to have a basic HTML home page. In order to compete in your industry, maybe you need to show off your creative side. For example, perhaps you're a graphic artist, an independent filmmaker, a cartoonist, or a musician. All these professions would benefit from a graphics-heavy or animated home page. In this case, I suggest creating a plain HTML version of your home page to submit to the search engines. This page can link to your more creative, flashy site. Make sure your plain home page includes an actual link to your Flash site rather than automatically redirecting the user. Automatic redirects are another huge pitfall for web rankings.

Redirects, pop-ups, and pop-unders

Redirects are a big red flag for search engines, mostly due to the pornography industry's abuse of the technology. If your URL redirects someone to another site automatically, the search engines assume you are hiding your real content and therefore will not rank you. Besides redirects, pop-ups can be equally devastating to your search positioning. However, the jury is still out on whether or not pop-unders are just as bad.

Pop-ups are advertisements that spawn a new web page in front of the current web page you are visiting, while pop-unders appear beneath your web browser. Pop-up ads are much more invasive, as they appear right in the middle of a particular web page, forcing you to acknowledge the ad by either clicking on it for more information or closing it completely before you can move on. Pop-unders appear after you have logged off a particular website.

Back buttons

Search engines such as Overture and Google will not sell ad space or keywords to websites that have disabled their browser back buttons. Other search engines are following suit, so it's important to keep your back buttons enabled, allowing users to return to the search engine.

Text links

In addition to reading the text on your site, search engine spiders pay extra attention to text links. The more keywords you can put within your text links the better. For example, rather than "Click here!" this is the perfect opportunity to add some keywords, such as "Click here for Discount Widgets." Search engines also look for text links to help them index your entire site. If your website only has graphic buttons for navigation, it will be very difficult for search engines to get past your home page and rank other pages within your site. Always add text-based navigation to your site. Text navigation can easily be added to the bottom footer of all pages within you site in addition to your regular, graphic-based navigation.

Site maps

Site maps are always a good idea. They not only help users find exactly what they are looking for, but they also help search engines index your website effectively, much in the same way text-based links do. Site maps are a way of outlining all the sections of your website in plain text. Search engines love site maps because they make categorizing each page and its content much easier. When creating your site map, link to as many specific product and service pages as possible within your site. In addition, be sure to link the entire product name, rather than adding a "click here" after the product name — it's the best way to help those individual product and service pages get indexed by the search spiders.

Frames

Frames are a search engine's worst nightmare. Luckily most web designers today are aware of this, so few sites are being designed with frames. Frames are essentially two (or sometimes more) web pages embedded in one another. Search engines pull one page at a time. So when a search engine is looking for information, it will pull pages out of their frames, causing loss of headers, footers, or important navigational features. Also, the way HTML code is written in frame-based websites hides the important content and keywords that search engines are looking for. Bottom line: get rid of your frames as soon as possible.

For best results, implement as many of the above strategies as possible. Many search engines follow a combination of these guidelines to determine ranking. The more your site content matches your site title, your site meta tags, and so on, the better your chance of holding a solid ranking in the top engines. The longer you hold these consistencies, the higher you will go.

Link Popularity

Link development should be a large piece of your search engine optimization plan. Top search engines such as Google determine which website to rank highest by how many incoming links it has. In other words, how popular the website is. The theory is that if other websites think your site is important and credible enough to link to, then it may be worth ranking higher than the other sites. The key to building successful link popularity is paying attention to the quality of sites that provide links to you, rather than the quantity. In other words, if you can get a link from a major news website, such as CNN.com or MSNBC.com, talking about your products and services, the link is weighed much more heavy than 100 links from small local business or hobby sites with no link popularity of their own. Taking time to build the right links is invaluable.

The first step to building a successful link popularity campaign is to visit a site like linkpopularity.com and see how many websites are already linking to you. Then enter in a few of your competitors sites' URLs and see who is linking to them. This will give you a good idea of how many links you may need to beat them in the search engine ranking game. It will also give you some good insight into what kind of partnerships and links they are getting, so you can see if it makes sense to contact those same websites.

Stay away from automated link exchange programs or web rings. The problem with these types of link development strategies is that Google will actually penalize a site with too many outgoing links. The idea is to have as many links as possible coming to your site, but limiting the number of links going out.

A great way to archive this is by becoming a content provider in your industry. Offer to write articles or provide content for other news sources or websites in your industry in exchange for giving you a byline and link to your website within the article. Along the same lines, online press releases are a great way to fuel your overall link popularity. Write a keyword-friendly press release about your company, product, or service and submit it to major news and PR services such as Google News, PRNewsWire, PRWeb, and others.

Resources for Search Engine Submission

Unfortunately, the days of the free search engine are long gone. Now all the remaining dot.coms are expected to turn a profit, even the search engines. Few search engine spiders will just stumble across your website. Today, you must hand submit your website along with your credit card number. Search engine registration fees can be anywhere from $19 to $299, and there is still no guarantee that your website will be listed. Therefore you need to follow the rules outlined in this chapter to ensure your search engine fees are well spent.

Microsoft's bCentral

Although hand-submission to the search engines is ideal, the best automated resource I have found for submission to the top search engines as well as hundreds of local engines is Microsoft's bCentral Submit It <www.bcentral.com> (also known as Microsoft Small Business Center). For about $49.95, bCentral provides you with the tools necessary to submit your site effectively to hundreds of engines. The best part about their Submit It tool is the "Readiness Check" feature. Before you can actually submit your site, you have to make sure it is "ready" to be submitted. The tool reviews your title tags, meta tags, and other necessities to ensure search engine success. You'll even get a full report on why your website passed or did not pass the readiness check, with directions on how to improve.

How Long Does It Take?

Getting to the top of the search engines is not an overnight process. In fact, even the most effectively optimized websites can end up in a "holding" period for several months before search engines will even index them. Many search engine marketers refer to this "holding" period as the "Sandbox Theory," and it most specifically applies to Google.

The Google Sandbox applies to all websites launched after March 2004. Despite how well optimized a site is, websites launched after that date are often not ranking well for their first few months live on the Internet. New websites are often placed on probation, and kept lower than expected in searches, prior to being given full value for optimization. The sandbox practice was implemented for a couple of different reasons, primarily having to do with making it difficult for search engine spammer sites to get ranked. Google wants to give more weight to long-term sites that will still be around in a year, rather than to sites that latch onto the latest search engine ranking tactic and essentially try to "cheat" their way to the top.

While all types of sites can be placed in the sandbox, the problem appears much more frequently for new websites seeking rankings for highly competitive keyword phrases and for sites that repeat specific keyword phrases too often (which can be considered search engine spam).

Once you are in the sandbox, only time can get your site out. However there are a few ways to speed up the process, which all go back to good website optimization — including strong keyword-friendly content and a solid link development strategy. It's also a good idea for business owners with new domain names to at least get something launched right away, rather than waiting for their site to look perfect or be completely finished. Even a basic informational page, letting users know that your full site will be launching soon, will help shorten your overall wait time.

Paying for Positioning

Waiting several months to get picked up by the search engines can cost you customers. Fortunately, there are now ways to jump ahead of the line with "pay-per-click positioning." Search engines such as FindWhat.com, Overture.com, and even Google allow advertisers to buy keywords to ensure that their company listing will show up whenever that word is searched.

Overture's pay-per-click program

After using all of these pay-for-positioning networks for a variety of clients, I've found the most success with Overture.com (changed to Yahoo! Search Marketing Solutions in March 2005). By purchasing one keyword on Overture, your website will automatically be listed at the top of Yahoo!, Lycos, MSN, AltaVista, Netscape, InfoSpace, CNet, and NetZero. The best part about Overture's "pay per click" ad model is you only pay when someone actually clicks through to your website. Overture also provides the tools necessary to monitor your own campaign 24 hours a day. By logging into your Overture account, you can easily see which words are giving you the most clicks and which ones might not be as effective. By using trackable URLs, you can even see which words are responsible for your online sales.

Google's AdWords Select program

Due to the importance Google places on long-term link popularity, it can be one of the most difficult search engines on which to get listed. Google is the top search engine right now, handling nearly double the search volume of Yahoo! Google does, however, offer a pay-for-positioning program called AdWords Select, which is slightly different from Overture's technology. I've found Google's AdWords Select program to be much more confusing to first-time Internet ad buyers than Overture's straightforward pay-per-click system. However, since Google is the top engine, it's worth the extra time and energy to figure out how to gain access to its large web audience.

Here's how Google's AdWords Select program works: rather than purchasing a simple keyword, you purchase banner ads that come up when your keyword group is searched. The frequency with which your banners appear depends on how much money you bid per keyword. The text banner, which you create yourself, is displayed on the right side of Google's regular listings. The problem? Banner ads typically do not have a high click-through rate, and are therefore just not as effective as having your listing show up in the regular content area of the site. (More on banner ads in the next chapter.) Google makes it more obvious which sites are paying for positioning, whereas Overture does a better job of making your paid listing appear more like a regular search result.

The other difficult part about Google's pay-for-positioning system is that, like any other form of media, Google is constantly trying to strike a balance between pleasing the marketers and generating revenue for themselves. As a result, Google's AdWord Select program forces marketers to work much harder than the straightforward keyword purchases. For example, if your banner ad does not generate an appropriate amount of click-throughs determined for that keyword, your banner will be removed from rotation. This concept clearly has its advantages and disadvantages. On the one hand, it forces marketers and website owners to create the most effective banner text to maximize click-throughs. On the other hand, it tends to put the banner ads purchased by the most experienced marketers on top, squeezing out the small-business owner short on time and resources.

Success with Keywords

With all pay-for-positioning programs, it takes simple trial and error to determine which words will turn into actual sales. The average Internet search is three words, which means savvy Internet users get very specific in their searches. For example, most people don't just search "real estate"; they would search "homes for sale in San Diego."

CPC versus CPM ad buys

It's hard to say just how much you should spend on keywords per month. This is something that varies with each industry and depends on what you wish to accomplish online. Search engine keywords are usually sold in one of two ways: on a CPM (cost per thousand impressions) or CPC (cost per click-through) basis. Pricing is then based on the popularity of the word, which is why I recommend getting as specific as possible. The more general the word, the more expensive it will be. Plus, general words earn a lot of wasted impressions and clicks, from people not looking for your product specifically.

Let's take the real estate example again. The keyword "real estate" is an extremely expensive one, and unless you are Century 21 buying keywords for its global office's website, there is really no reason to purchase this keyword. A local real estate agent is better off getting more specific.

The use of landing pages

It's a good idea to specify a specific URL with your keyword buy. This will ensure your visitors will find exactly what they are looking for right away. These customized web pages designed to close the sale on users who click on a specific ad are called "landing pages." By creating pages specific to what the user was searching for, then testing various offers and text on those pages, your conversion rate will be even higher. Purchasing keywords is the most effective ad buy available, but it is easy to waste a lot of money if you don't take the extra steps to customize the results users will see when they click through to your site.

Writing effective ad copy

Just as important as the keywords you buy is the ad copy you include with that keyword. Both Google and Overture allow advertisers to specify the ad copy or title tag that will appear when a keyword is searched. By customizing your ad copy to the specific keywords, you will maximize your chance of quality click-throughs.

Once you are a regular advertiser with Google or Overture, you can edit your keywords, ad text, and URLs as often as you like — which means you can run different keyword campaigns at different times of the year, month, or even daily. For example, if you

Take some time writing the ad copy to include with your keyword. The copy can be as important as the keyword itself.

buy the keyword phrase "Bridesmaid dress," you can run the descriptive text "50% off on all Bridesmaid dresses in July," which can take the person to a landing page with the coupon.

Promotions and coupons help your listing stand out from the rest. But be careful not to overuse punctuation or capital letters. Both Google and Overture won't accept ad copy that is too strong. Paid listings are meant to be read, like editorial, not advertisements. Therefore, your ad copy will be rejected if you use superlative words like "best." Also, if you choose to use an offer or promotion as your ad copy, it must be a legitimate offer. Google won't let you use the word "free" unless your landing page actually gives away something for free. If it's a "buy one, get one free" type of promotion, you must specify this before the person clicks. In other words, no misleading ads.

If you think you've seen ads on Google or Overture that break these rules, it's because once you are a regular advertiser, your ads can go live instantly after you post an edit. But be assured that as soon as the search engine staff gets a chance to review your ad copy, it will be pulled if it doesn't follow the guidelines. The pay-for-positioning guidelines are just that, guidelines. They are constantly changing to make the buys most effective for both searchers and marketers, so be sure to read the latest rules posted on Google and Overture before you write your ad copy.

To sum up, gaining new web traffic is more than adding the right tags and registering for the right search engines. It is a combination of all of the ideas and concepts outlined in this book to expand your overall web presence. Websites such as Google and Yahoo! recognize the most popular websites and tend to rank them higher in the long run. Yahoo! and Google determine a website's popularity by how many other quality websites are linked to them. In the end, the more web content you exchange with others in your industry and the more product links you get on other sites, the more this will help your overall web traffic. The more places your website address is found on the Internet, the better your chances of being found by the search engines.

Use Worksheet 4 to help you determine if your site is search-engine ready.

Worksheet 4
SEARCH ENGINE SUBMISSION READINESS CHECK

Is your website ready to be submitted to the search engines? Take the test below before you proceed.

Define one to three keyword phrases that people would use to find your product or service. (A phrase must be longer than one word.)

1. _____

2. _____

3. _____

For your website to be optimized for the above keyword phrases, you must be able to check every box below.

❑ The above keyword phrase(s) shows up in my home page text (not graphics) at least three times.

❑ The above keyword phrase(s) shows up at least once in the first sentence on my home page.

❑ The above keyword phrase(s) shows up in my website's title tag. (Look at the top of the browser window to verify.)

❑ The above keyword phrase(s) shows up in my website's meta tags. (This will be in the HTML code. Ask your web designer.)

❑ The above keyword phrase(s) shows up in my website's description tags. (This will be in the HTML code. Ask your web designer to verify.)

❑ The above keyword phrase(s) shows up in my website's ALT tags. (Roll your mouse over your graphics to see which keywords come up.)

If you can check off all the above boxes (and you haven't committed any of the web design pitfalls described in this chapter or chapter 10), you are ready to submit your website to the search engines.

CHAPTER 9

BUYING TRAFFIC THROUGH BANNER ADS

So far, I've talked about ways to generate free and low-cost advertising for your website through search engine optimization, content development, and co-branding strategies. Ad buys can also be an important part of your online marketing campaign; however, they can also be the most expensive part of your plan and generate the least return on investment.

CPM, CPC, and CPA Ad Buys

As when buying keywords, it's difficult to say just how much you should budget per month for online ad buys, for this will depend on your industry and what you are trying to accomplish online. Online advertisements, such as banners, are most commonly sold in three ways:

- ◗ CPM (cost per thousand impressions)
- ◗ CPA (cost per action or cost per sale)
- ◗ CPC (cost per click-through)

On both a CPM or CPC ad buy, it's important to get as specific as possible. For example, don't buy banner ads on home pages of general websites, but rather on specific pages that relate to your product. Doing so saves money and generates more targeted leads.

Banner advertising can be expensive. Choose the sites on which your banner will appear based on their target market, not their overall traffic.

Your online advertising buys should always be about profit over volume. In other words, always opt for lower traffic solutions that offer a higher profit margin. The more general the web page your ad is on, the more expensive it will be. Remember the story of our first ad buy for our Baja website? We purchased a banner ad on the Yahoo! Travel page. Our 100,000 impressions were completed in less than a day, our click-through rate was at an all-time low, and the buy produced exactly zero sales.

For businesses on a tight budget, I recommend going with a CPC (cost-per-click-through) model. CPC buys ensure that you are paying only for actual traffic to your website. Many times, as with an Overture.com ad buy, you can set your monthly budget ahead of time, so you only get as many clicks as you have budgeted. This feature lets you stick with what you feel comfortable spending, so you can get a true feel of what type of investment you are looking at.

Of course, the most effective ad buy is a CPA (cost per action or cost per sale); however, it is difficult to find large companies and search engines willing to work out that kind of deal with a small business. Again, it's really a question of trial and error to know which type of buy is best for your business and industry. But the great thing about all three types of ad buys is that the results are completely trackable. Trackable results mean that over time you'll be able to refine and better plan your campaign.

Testing, Testing, Testing

No matter what type of ad buy you choose, testing is key. It's a good idea to test multiple different messages and designs at the same time. Most websites allow you to upload two to three different banners. Testing is always wise, because no matter how well you think you know your audience, sometimes the most unpredictable banners will generate the most response.

For example, when we launched the JennyCraig.com banner ad campaign across <www.iVillage.com> and other top women's websites, we were surprised to learn that the banner ads that did not include the Jenny Craig logo or brand name gained the most clicks. The banner ads that were more general to weight loss proved most successful. The theory behind the success of the more general banners over the branded ones was that when people saw the Jenny Craig brand name, they assumed that they already knew everything about the company, so why click? In contrast, the general weight loss banner ads, which featured advice or questions, generated much more interest because they appeared to offer a new solution to the age-old problem. The banner ad that proved most successful of the entire campaign featured a woman sunbathing, with the question "Wanna find out how to make your ex-boyfriend jealous this summer?"

The banner worked for three reasons:

(a) It was timely. The ad ran at the beginning of summer, when dieters start thinking most about bathing suit season.

(b) It asked a question. Banner ads with questions get more clicks because they engage the reader.

(c) It featured a picture of a woman. Banner ads featuring pictures of people, especially close-ups of faces, gain more clicks than other banner designs.

Often, the most effective banner ad is one that asks the viewer a question.

How to Make a Banner Ad Successful

Here are some additional rules to follow when making online ad buys:

(a) *Show immediate benefit.* Let the potential buyer know right away why they should click on your ad.

(b) *Specify the action you want the user to take.* Click here! Call now!

(c) *Attract the user's attention.* Words such as "free," pictures of faces, or flashy animation all tend to do the trick.

(d) *Choose your words carefully.* Don't waste the small space you have for your ad message with words like "welcome," "online," "website," or "home page." They are considered so common that they convey little meaning. In fact, Google won't even let you use these words in banner ads on their website, unless they are essential to describing your product, like "website hosting" or "online marketing seminar."

(e) *Encourage the consumer to act.* Small businesses should never buy banners for general branding purposes. It is just too expensive. Instead, create banners that encourage the user to take a specific action, whether it's to sign up for your contest or a 30-day trial of your service. Then measure the results of that ad with your web tracking software.

(f) *Test multiple designs.* Always test different messages and designs at the same time. Most websites allow you to upload two to three different banners during one campaign cycle.

(g) *Create a complementary web page.* Don't make a visitor who just clicked through your banner ad hunt through your website for the same promotion. Send visitors directly to a page designed specifically to complement that banner ad promotion. You will have a much better chance of closing the deal. Follow this rule for keyword ad buys as well. (To find out how *Men's Health* put this principle to work in a successful banner ad campaign, see the Case Study at the end of this chapter.)

Why Banner Ads Are Not Cost-Effective

Overall, banner ads have not proved to be the most effective way to generate traffic, especially ROS (run-of-site) banners. For online marketers, if your banner ad generates a 2 percent to 5 percent click-through rate, it is considered above average. That isn't a whole lot of return on investment. In addition, eMarketer released the following statistics about banner ads:

 ▶ The vast majority (99 percent) of banners don't get clicked on.

 ▶ Almost half (49 percent) of users don't even look at banners.

My advice to small businesses looking to the Internet to market their services is to heed the marketing suggestions in chapters 1 to 8 and the web design advice in chapters 10 and 11. Most online ad buys, especially banners, are just not cost-effective for small businesses. And the more that marketers and businesses begin to understand that there are different ways to get your message across on the Internet, the less you'll see of banners in the coming years.

Stick to Highly Targeted Campaigns

Rather than spending your valuable marketing dollars on an online advertisement, spend a little extra time building relationships and swapping content with other websites. No matter what industry you are in, highly targeted, direct messages continue to be the key to cost-effective online marketing. And permission-based e-mail programs remain the most efficient way for small businesses to send these targeted messages.

Search engine optimization offers an equally effective way to put your product in front of a captive audience that is actively searching for your product or service. With that said, keywords are the most targeted form of online advertising you can buy.

Track Results

The key to a successful online ad buy is return on investment. Determine what exactly would define an effective ad buy for your company, whether it is 20,000 more visitors per month or 200 more e-mail addresses. Then test, test, test to determine what works best to reach those goals. Don't depend on the advertiser statistics and results the seller gives you to track the success of your campaign. These stats can often be misleading. Instead, use your own web traffic programs, such as LiveStats, Urchin, or Web Trends, to read the data.

When you use your own resources, the results will be more consistent and you'll get a better idea of which ad buys are actually working. Besides, you'll want to know more detailed information than how many people clicked on your advertisement. You'll want to know which ads actually encouraged visitors to take a specified action on your site. Online advertising should be about more than generating web traffic; it should be about generating real results for your business.

Fresh content is essential to any campaign. If you can generate content for the top sites in your industry, you may have a way to get some free advertising for your business.

CASE STUDY

When the popular men's fitness magazine *Men's Health* launched its banner ad campaign in 2000, it captured more than 100,000 of its 1.2 million paid subscribers. The success of the campaign can be attributed to four primary factors: design, content, placement, and timing.

The design and content of the banner ads followed the same editorial feel of the magazine's covers. As Ed Fones, senior vice president and managing director of Men's Health Group World Wide, told Stephanie Clifford in her January 2001 *eCompany Now* article, "We have to deliver the creative in a benefit-oriented way — get abs like these, have the best sex of your life tonight, lose 10 pounds — a lot of things you'd see as cover lines on the magazine."

The banner ads all targeted men's desire to be sexier, healthier, and fit, along with the need to understand and appeal to the opposite sex. They proved wildly successful, generating more than 6,000 unique visitors to <www.Menshealth.com> per month. But it's one thing to encourage click-throughs, and quite another to actually turn those clicks into quality leads.

"We have recently toned down our more sensationalistic banners dealing with sex in an attempt to pull in more qualified visitors," Kevin Labick, the creative director for Menshealth.com banner ads, told ChannelSeven.com. "I never write ads to promote a site; instead I focus on the specific services the site has to offer. Menshealth.com is a comprehensive site that addresses every aspect of a man's life. The banners speak to guys with a brotherly voice. They identify the goals of men and then link them to features that help them attain those goals."

Placement of the banner ads on top men's sites such as <www.ESPN.com> and <www.Playboy.com> and on related pages on the search engines AltaVista and Yahoo! contributed to the banners' high conversion rate, as did Menshealth.com's subscription-centric website. Every banner ad linked to a web page article framed with magazine offers enticing users to sign up for a subscription or request a free trial.

The banners combined appealing content with a sense of urgency. For example, they promoted gift ideas and reminded viewers to buy their girlfriends flowers for upcoming special occasions such as Valentine's Day. Seasonal banners that relate to a specific holiday or time of year prove more successful than more general promotions.

The *Men's Health* banners generate about 35 percent of the magazine's online subscriptions. According to Clifford, grabbing this many new subscribers by direct mail would cost well over $2 million.

CHAPTER 10
BASICS OF GOOD WEB DESIGN

Even the most innovative and expensive ad buys will get a visitor to your website only once. After that, it's the content and design of your site that keeps people coming back for more and turns visitors into lasting customers.

Simple Sites Are Best

No matter how sophisticated Internet technology becomes, our favorite sites have always been the ones with the best information and easiest navigation. AOL, Yahoo!, Amazon, and eBay continue to enjoy success, because they are so easy to use. Yahoo! has simple graphics and a mostly text-based interface, but people log on again and again for its fast downloading content and easy-to-use home page. Unless you're in the entertainment or technology industry, people are not expecting the newest web applications, heavy downloads, audio, or video. These extras usually just slow things down and get in the way of the real content.

However this is not to say that your website should be boring. Just as a great magazine cover or brochure does, capture the user's attention with great images, photos, and well-written text. And most important, let a visitor know right away the answer to the question "What's in it for me?"

Keep the User in Mind

Among the most important principles of web design is to keep your site simple.

Tom Hespos had the right idea when he penned "How My Mom Uses the Web," his December 1998 *ClickZ* article. To get an honest opinion of how effective and easy to use your website is, have someone outside your office, such as a friend or family member, click through it. Take notes on where they click and how long they remain in each area. Then interview them about your site. Did they understand each link? What kind of feeling did they get when they first saw your home page? How would they define your product and your company values based on your website? Do they see a reason to go back and visit again?

Guidelines for Effective Web Design

Besides easy-to-use web pages, how else can you keep your existing audience loyal and encourage newer visitors to come back for more? Start by reviewing the following guidelines for effective website design:

(a) *Be consistent throughout the site.* Using the same font or color schemes breeds familiarity and comfort for visitors when they navigate through a site. Also, don't underline anything unless it's a link. Doing so is confusing to the user.

(b) *Follow editorial standards.* Broken links and typos make your site lose credibility. Take time to proof all your updates and stories with the same care you would give a piece going to print.

(c) *Don't focus all your attention on the home page.* Search engines can send visitors to any page of your site.

(d) *Test your site on all platforms and browsers.* Just because everyone in your office uses the latest version of Internet Explorer on a PC, don't assume the rest of the world does. Your website can look drastically different on another monitor or browser. And don't forget AOL. Web developers tend to overlook this still very large audience.

(e) *Aim for fast downloading.* Fast downloading is more important to most Internet users than flashy animation. Remember, just because you can make something flashy doesn't mean you should. If you do choose to use large files, provide a basic text version of your website as well. Not everyone has high-speed Internet access. Your office computer connection is probably about 40 percent faster than that of the typical home user.

(f) *Create a designated spot on your home page to showcase new content.* If you keep new content in the same designated area, repeat visitors hoping to find the same information they found before won't be confused by the change. Also, it's a good idea to date new content; this encourages new visitors to visit your site again to see something new. Updating a website is much cheaper than updating a brochure or any other type of print material. Take advantage of the web by using it to test new promotions.

Be certain your visitors find your website easy to use.

(g) *Always provide a link back home.* No matter where visitors end up on a site, they should easily be able to return to the home page. If your site provides links to other URLS, don't lose visitors by not giving them a quick path back to your site. Creating an extra browser window or mini frame are both good ways to keep visitors from straying too far.

(h) *Get to the point.* New visitors should be able to find out exactly what your company or product can do for them in less than 15 seconds. Everything on your home page should help new customers make the decision to buy your product.

(i) *Encourage viral marketing.* Remember to include strategically placed "e-mail a friend" links or other content that gets people talking about your product.

(j) *Get visitors' e-mail addresses.* Create an environment that encourages users to give you their e-mail address. Remember, creating a database of names and gathering information about your customer base is one of the reasons you publish a website. Give users an option to be included on your mailing list. Then e-mail coupons, links to news updates, and press releases — anything that will spark some interest and keep them coming back for more.

Sticking to these basic rules of web design is essential to ensuring repeat customers and getting the most out of your website. Go through this list with your web designer to make sure you are both on the same page. Remember, the goal of your website is to help your business and attract more customers, not to impress other web designers.

Worksheet 5 and Worksheet 6 can help you determine your site's usability and marketability.

Worksheet 5
TESTING YOUR WEBSITE FOR USABILITY

Chapter 10 examines the importance of having people outside your company look at your website to test it for usability. Below is a list of questions you should give to your family and friends as they look at your website. Remember to test people with different levels of Internet experience to make sure your website makes sense to all types of customers.

1. What type of browser are you using to view this website? (check one)

    ❑ Internet Explorer

    ❑ Netscape Navigator

    ❑ AOL

    ❑ Other: _____

2. What type of computer are you using?

    ❑ Mac

    ❑ PC

3. What is your connection speed?

    ❑ Dial up

    ❑ Cable Modem

    ❑ DSL

    ❑ T1

    ❑ Other: _____

4. How fast did the website come up?

5. What is the purpose of this website?

6. What service or product is this company selling?

7. If the website has a shopping cart, try to buy something, and rate your overall experience from 1 to 5 (1 = great experience, 5 = confusing). If the shopping cart was confusing, explain why.

8. How would you contact someone at this company if you had more questions? Can you easily find a phone number and an e-mail address?

9. For what type of person do you think this website was built?

10. Do you see a reason to return to this website?

11. Is this website missing anything? Is there anything you would like to see more of?

12. What is your overall feeling about this website?

13. Would you recommend this website's services/product to anyone? If yes, to whom would you recommend it?

14. List your favorite websites below and briefly explain why they are your favorites.

    (a) _____

    (b) _____

    (c) _____

Worksheet 6
RATE YOUR WEBSITE'S MARKETABILITY

The preceding chapters have examined different online marketing campaigns and web design strategies to attract both new and repeat customers. Take the test below to see if your site is ready for an online marketing campaign!

1. There is a designated place on your home page to showcase new content and/or promotions.

   ❑ True

   ❑ False

2. Your contact information (both phone number and e-mail address) are prominently displayed at the bottom of the home page and any product pages.

   ❑ True

   ❑ False

3. Your website encourages users to sign up for your e-mail mailing list or offer their contact information.

   ❑ True

   ❑ False

4. Your website encourages viral marketing through "e-mail a friend" links or interesting content, design, or promotions that would spark word-of-mouth.

   ❑ True

   ❑ False

5. Your website gives users a special incentive to buy online through special discounts, coupons, or other promotions.

   ❑ True

   ❑ False

6. You are able to respond to customer inquiries within 24 to 48 hours.

   ❑ True

   ❑ False

7. You have the ability to monitor your website's traffic. (You can track how many visitors your site receives each day.)

   ❑ True

   ❑ False

For each True answer, give yourself 1 point. Then rank your website according to the scale below:

0 to 2 points = Stop! Don't waste money on online marketing campaigns before your website is up to speed. Implement at least four of the above site features to get the most out of your online marketing efforts.

3 to 4 points = Average. Your website needs work. Adding a few more of the above options will dramatically improve your site's chances of success.

5 to 7 points = Excellent! You are ready to start a full online marketing campaign.

CHAPTER 11

WORKING WITH YOUR WEB DEVELOPER

I've been on both ends of the phone. I've been the client desperately trying to get our outside web designers to create the right template before we dashed off to the big snowboarding event <www.twsnow.com/> for which we were providing live coverage. I've endured the frustrating calls to an account manager with no technical background and even less authority. I've experienced the vague time estimates and the infamous time zone differences that can make getting what I need before my deadlines a reoccurring nightmare.

Using an outside web agency or designer can be frustrating. But if you know how to ask the right questions, your web developer can become your business's most valuable asset. Here are a few words of advice to enhance all your online relationships.

Stay Away from Technical Lingo

Even if you know exactly what you want, explain it to your web developer in nontechnical terms. After all, that's why you hired a professional in the first place: they probably know of a more effective way to get your ideas across.

Be Prepared and Define Your Goals

Always keep your business goals in mind in discussions with your web designer, and make certain he or she understands your goals as well.

Nothing wastes more time than a client who doesn't know what he or she wants. Take time before each call or meeting with your web developer to think of the long- and short-term outcomes of any changes to design or strategy you may be requesting. Most web designers will do exactly what you tell them, without considering the possible outcomes to your business goals. It is your responsibility to make sure any design changes or content additions adhere to your overall business goals; it is the web designer's job to make sure the changes or additions are displayed the best possible way on the web. In other words, don't expect your web designer to make business decisions for you.

However, do remind your web developer what your overall business goal is. It will keep him or her moving quickly in the right direction. It also helps you to stay focused on the big picture and nail down exactly what your company is trying to accomplish by making adjustments to the website.

Use Examples of Other Sites

Have some examples of websites you like and dislike. And be specific about what it is you like and don't like about those sites. This goes for web developers as well. Give your clients some ideas to take back to the office. Click through their competitors' sites and give insight into what works and what doesn't for their industry.

Get 24/7 Tech Support

Don't wait for a crisis to erupt before learning that your primary contact is away at an off-site meeting. Because website disasters happen in real time, make sure your web developer offers 24/7 tech support. Just because your website goes down after 5:00 p.m. is no excuse for your hosting company or web designer not to get it back up and running right away. If you are using an independent web designer rather than an agency, always get an emergency after-hours contact number and find out who your secondary contact is in case your primary contact is unavailable.

Put Everything in Writing

After an initial phone call in which new projects are discussed, always follow up with a detailed e-mail explaining what you want. Having things in writing leaves less room for interpretation between two parties and saves everyone time in the long run.

Keep Your Developer Informed

Your web development team has only as much information about your industry and your company's online goals as you tell them. Keep them updated with what's going on in your company and with your competitors. It's their job to come up with ways to promote your site and keep people coming back for more. It's your job to make sure those ideas make sense for your budget and your business goals.

The Price of Web Design

As of the time this book goes to press, the price of web development ranges from $25 to $75 per hour for an independent web designer and $60 to $150 per hour for an agency web designer. Agencies can cost you a lot of money, since you often have to pay for a third-party account manager to manage the project. However, working with an agency allows you to pull from a larger talent pool of professional designers and online marketers, ensuring the exact look and feel you want. Independent web designers are more flexible on pricing, which can save you a lot money. However, they can also be more flexible on contracts and deadlines, which can cause problems

No matter what type of web developer you go with, be sure to get letters of recommendation and ask if you can contact some of their past clients as references. It is so important to choose a quality web designer that you can get along with on a personal as well as a professional level, because as your company grows, you will come to depend on your web designer more and more.

Creating and maintaining a website shouldn't be a struggle. The number of web development agencies and independent web designers is rising rapidly, and they all want your business. If you feel that you are not getting the most out of your current web developer, it's probably time to look for a new one.

CHAPTER 12

THE POWER OF THE WEB

There's a place 14 hours down the coast of Baja where the roads aren't paved, houses don't have plumbing, and the only telephone resides in the town post office. But they asked me to build a website for them.

The town is called Punta Abreojos, and the local fishermen are concerned with the state of their industry and a changing environment. Big businesses are moving in. Although most of the locals don't even own a television, they understand the power of the web. They see the Internet as an opportunity for people in any social or economic class to get their message to the rest of the world. And they're right.

The Internet Reaches Everyone

Publishing is no longer a business of the rich. In the mid-1990s the Internet was repeatedly referred to as "the great equalizer," a way that small businesses could finally compete with the Fortune 500 companies.

Crossing the economic barrier

Almost anyone can get a free e-mail account through Hotmail or a basic website through Yahoo! GeoCities <geocities.yahoo.com>. There are now even free ISP services, such as NetZero <www.netzero .net>, the only cost being a little junk e-mail and some well-placed advertisements. And for those who can't afford a computer, more and more high-speed Internet cafés are showing up in rural towns around the world.

The web makes it possible for everyone to access information. It is now easier than ever to get your message out and attract customers.

The web is accomplishing the very thing that TV was once recognized for. It provides information to the lower and middle classes that was once available only to those who were well traveled, well educated, or well financed. In fact, the web has taken on this role and pushed it to another level. Consider, on the one hand, that viewers passively watch television, whose content is created by a select few. Web surfers, on the other hand, are an active part of the process. The web is something people actively seek out and can interact with. You don't have to be beautiful or wealthy to get your message across on the web.

Breaking the language barrier

Besides crossing the economic barrier, the web has broken the language barrier as well. Technology allows web pages to be converted to other languages through browser tools and web-based applications. But until translation technology is perfected, many companies are creating their own translations. BMW lets users choose between English and German, while large portals such as Yahoo! offer entirely different versions of their website for each part of the world. More and more companies recognize the web as a tool to gain access to the international market.

What do browser-based translation software, free e-mail, free websites, and the rapid growth of Internet cafés say about the future of the web? They show that even poorer countries can be big targets for online marketing plans and e-commerce. In rural areas of the world, people see more reliability in e-mailing their friends and family from a local Internet café than in depending on the local postal services. Even those in metropolitan areas use e-mail for the pure speed over traditional mail. We all know that e-mail is a more cost-effective alternative to picking up the phone, especially when doing business overseas. For foreign shoppers, the

Internet gives users direct access to US fashions and trends that may not be available in their local shops.

What this means for your small business

So what does all this have to do with your small business? It should get you thinking about all of the markets out there that the web can provide access and insight to. Don't just focus on the upper-class or tech-savvy group. There is a reason it's called the web, remember? It's the one medium that truly transcends language, social, and economic barriers. It's a tangled network viewed and created by all types of people. In turn, it gives you, the marketer, insight and information about those people in a way that no other medium ever has.

What a big business can do with deep pockets and great resources, a small business can do with passion, creativity, and planning.

Today, more than ever, it is easy to get discouraged by the deep pockets of big business. Big businesses have the resources to hire entire marketing departments with expertise in search engine optimization and online ad buys. They have full-time creative teams dreaming up flashing home pages and professional photographers capturing their celebrity spokesperson. Yet the big guys don't have the same passion, drive, and emotional investment a small-business entrepreneur does. Although big businesses can throw hundreds of thousands of dollars into an online ad campaign just to test the waters, small businesses need to see a direct return on investment on every dollar spent, or they won't be around in a month to try another campaign. Yet a well-thought-out web campaign driven by someone who truly cares about the company, product, and customer can be just as effective as a large-scale campaign.

Key Points about Online Marketing

The following four points sum up the ideas covered in this book. Stick to these guidelines and you will see success in your online marketing campaign, no matter what your budget.

(a) *Maximize the conversion rate on your website.* Every story, image, and link should drive a visitor to your overall web goal. Eliminate any frivolous graphics or information that does not directly encourage the customer to take the action you want. Monitor your web traffic reports regularly to make sure visitors are clicking where you have intended them to click. Keep modifying your site until you get the results you want.

(b) *Trade volume for profitability.* Get as targeted as possible on keyword and banner buys. Buying very general keywords such as "real estate" or banners on popular home pages such as Yahoo! or MSN is a waste of money. General branding is much too expensive for any small business. Don't try to compete with the big guys this way, because you'll never be able to keep up. Instead look for a side door to your target market. Always opt for lower traffic solutions that offer a higher profit margin.

(c) *Celebrate the fact that you are a small business.* Rather than hiding the nature of your business, tell customers right away why they can benefit from using your company's service rather than a big business. Will they get faster service? More attention to detail? More personality? Better customer service? Many people want to support the small-business owner, but they still need to know right away what is in it for them.

(d) *Use e-mail to keep the communication lines open with potential customers.* It is a cheap way to follow up, send coupons, and encourage repeat business as well as to find new business through viral marketing.

Small businesses truly can compete with the big guys online. So be creative, pay attention to upcoming trends, and make the web your business's most powerful marketing tool.

REFERENCES

The links for the following references are provided on the CD-ROM in the References section.

Aaronson, Jack. "Zero-Budget Personalization Makeover, No.1: A Small Travel Agent." *ClickZ,* March 21, 2002.

Anderson, Heidi. "Email Testing: Here Come the Bridesmaids." *ClickZ,* April 18, 2002.

Bush, Michael. "Toyota 4Runner Reaches Heights with Everest Tie-In." *DMNews.com,* September 24, 2002.

Channel Seven. "Case Studies: MensHealth.com." Cited February 9, 2003.

Clifford, Stephanie. "Case Studies: MensHealth.com." *eCompany Now,* January 2001.

CommerceNet/Nielsen Media Research.

"Cover Story: Generation Y." *Business Week,* February 15, 1999.

Crosbie, Vin. "Lies, Damn Lies, and Statistics." *ClickZ,* August 13, 2002.

DoubleClick and Information Resources. "IRI and DoubleClick Study Shows Online
  Advertising Drives Sales of Consumer Packaged Goods Brands." April 10, 2002.

Edison Media Research and Arbitron. "TV in the New Media World." 2001.

Eisenberg, Bryan. "RE: Email Subject Lines That Work?" *ClickZ*, May 21, 2002.

eMarketer. Statistics.

Forrester Research. "Consumer Technographics North America Report." October 2001.

——. "Online Seniors: A Growing But Cautious Group." July 24, 2001.

Gaffney, John. "Case Study: Corn Syrup, Britney, the Web, and Thou." *Business 2.0,*
  August 2001.

——. "Forget the New M3. BMW's Hottest Product Is Streaming Online." *Business 2.0,*
  August 2001.

Gartner Group. "Community Technologies: Something Old, Something New."
  July 2, 2001.

Halfin, Bobbie. "Case Studies for Innovative Branding: Fashion." *ClickZ,* May 20, 1999.

——. "Case Studies for Innovative Web Branding: Credit Cards." *ClickZ,* March 11, 1999.

Hespos, Tom. "How My Mom Uses the Web." *ClickZ,* December 15, 1998.

Hopper, Ian. " 'ILOVEYOU' Computer Bug Bites Hard, Spreads Fast." CNN.com,
  May 4, 2000.

Lieb, Rebecca. "Smoking Out Online Buyers." *ClickZ,* August 23, 2002.

Lindstrom, Martin. "Big Brand, Zero Bucks." *ClickZ,* August 6, 2002.

——. "Brand Alliances Put to the Test." *ClickZ,* May 14, 2002.

——. "Brand + Brand = Success? Part 1." *ClickZ,* March 5, 2002.

———. "Brand + Brand = Success? Part 2: Brand Marriage Failure." *ClickZ,* March 12, 2002.

———. "Home Page Monotony." *ClickZ,* April 9, 2002.

Lithium Technologies. "Customer Reach Communities." October 20, 2002.

Magill, Ken. "Half of Net Users Will Buy Online in 2002: eMarketer." *DMNews.com,* April 18, 2002.

———. "Travel Sites Surge in March." *DMNews.com,* April 18, 2002.

Market Wire. "Guerilla Marketing in the Internet Age: Professional, Behavioral, Viral and Direct Marketing Basics." August 13, 2002.

Mulcahy, Seana. "Teaching New Dogs Old Tricks." *ClickZ,* September 17, 2002.

Parker, Pamela. "What's Critical in Cross Media? Online." *ClickZ,* February 8, 2002.

Peterson, Kim. "Jack Abbott: Five Questions." *SignOnSanDiego.com,* August 26, 2002.

Reynolds, Rob. "On Solid Ground." *Inc Magazine,* November 15, 1999.

Saunders, Christopher. "Study: Web Leads in Reaching Business Execs." *ClickZ,* September 9, 2002.

Solomon, Susan. "Content Winners (No Recount Required)." *ClickZ,* January 30, 2001.

———. "Set Your Sites on Seniors." *ClickZ,* June 11, 2002.

Sullivan, Danny. "Death of a Meta Tag." *ClickZ,* October 9, 2002.

Swack, Terry. "Case Study: Sephora.com." Internet World, December 15, 2000.

Weil, Debbie. "Crafting an Effective B2B Subject Line." *ClickZ,* February 21, 2001.

Yankee Group. "Internet Survey." 2002.

The CD-ROM includes the following worksheets for use on a Windows-based PC. The following forms are included in MS Word and PDF formats:

- Discovering Your Target Audience
- Planning Your E-Mail Campaign
- Finding the Right Co-Branding Partner
- Search Engine Submission Readiness Check
- Testing Your Website for Usability
- Rate Your Website's Marketability

The CD-ROM also includes links to the articles listed in the References section of this book.